P9-EGM-695

7th Edition

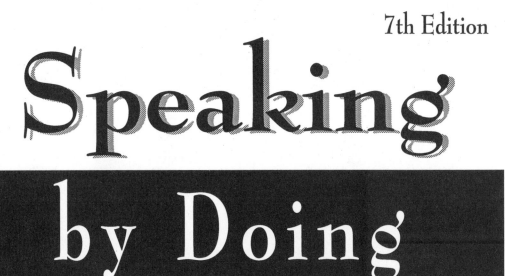

Speaking by Doing

A Speaking-Listening Text

Joseph A. Quattrini

National Textbook Company
NTC a division of *NTC Publishing Group* • Lincolnwood, Illinois USA

Dedicated to the late William E. Buys, who served as the author of the previous editions.

Published by National Textbook Company, a division of NTC Publishing Group.
©1996, 1991, 1986, 1981, 1973, 1967, 1960 by NTC Publishing Group, 4255 West Touhy Avenue,
Lincolnwood (Chicago), Illinois 60646–1975 U.S.A.
Manufactured in the United States of America.

5 6 7 8 9 ML 0 9 8 7 6 5 4 3 2 1

CONTENTS

TO THE TEACHER

"Reading, writing, and arithmetic"—What's wrong with this list? The list is incomplete because it leaves out speaking and listening, the means we use to communicate most of what we have to "say," and most of what is "said" to us. Oral communication is important in all aspects of our lives.

Thinking with language involves using symbols—placeholders for things and ideas in the universe. These thoughts are most often expressed through speech and apprehended by others through listening. Further, language is a kind of "self-talk," or symbolic processing. Through talk with others and self-talk, a knowing self is developed. Just as we communicate externally with others, we communicate internally with ourselves.

Speaking and listening are also the activities that occupy the majority of the academic day for learners and teachers in high school and college. Decisions by groups ranging from individual families to the United Nations General Assembly are reached after exploring issues and alternatives through means of discussion and debate.

More than ever, oral language abilities are requirements for career success. More than ever, interpersonal communication skills are in demand. The electronic age, the information age, and the communication age are virtually synonymous. Nearly 86 percent of all careers today are service-connected, and service industries depend on people talking to one another to conduct business.

Electronic media—radio, television, audiotapes, videotapes, the telephone, compact discs, and other forms of media—depend wholly or in part on speaking and listening. Computers are now able to process voice commands as well as keystrokes.

Conversation isn't really a lost art, and the language abilities of speaking and listening are as important as ever to the individual and the group in personal, social, academic, and work settings.

The speech course is an opportunity for your students to develop these crucial speaking and listening abilities. The course is your opportunity to encourage and guide their development.

This new edition of *Speaking by Doing* recognizes the need for more attention to oral communication. It recognizes the need for adapting to the rapid changes of society. It recognizes the need for all persons to participate if we are to have a strong and viable society. The new features of the text and this resource book—the Speaking and Listening Portfolio, the Portfolio Progress Report, the Chapter Checkup Questions, and the Speaker's Forum Project—all reflect these needs.

—J. A. Q.

Part One
Using the Text

OVERVIEW

The motivation for the approach to teaching speech, exemplified by the text, derives from the work of John Dewey, particularly his *Democracy and Education*, and *How We Learn*. It also has been stimulated by the belief of the authors that reading or talking about something, although it has value, does not change student behaviors. To be actively involved in one's learning is a *sine qua non* of effective education. This basic assumption led to the title of the text, *Speaking by Doing*. This edition continues the basic premises of the earlier editions.

In a school setting where a qualified speech communication teacher and a library of speech communication materials are available, *Speaking by Doing* can be used as a course outline that structures, logically and psychologically, sequential learning experiences. It is expected that available reading from the community's libraries and help from the teacher and the community's citizens will flesh out the content of each chapter.

In a school where the speech teacher has had limited professional training, or has meager support in learning resources, this text provides ample information for the development of concepts and skills related to public speaking and to listening. *Speaking by Doing* can be used successfully as the main text for an introductory course in speech communication.

There are important differences in this seventh edition. First, the text has been reorganized into these sections:

1. Why We Speak

2. Preparing and Presenting

3. Speaking for Personal Expression and Interpretation

4. Speaking for Information and Demonstration

5. Speaking for Persuasion and Problem Solving

6. Preparing and Presenting Your Portfolio

In brief, Section 1 shows the *why* of speaking and listening; Section 2 shows the *how*. Sections 3 to 5 give specific applications, and Section 6 measures growth and development. The Section Preview summarizes each section, and the Chapter Challenge creates focus for the main activity of each chapter.

The second major change is the portfolio. In this edition, all the materials and assignments for creating a Speaking and Listening Portfolio are included in the student text: goals, self-assessments, Building Your Portfolio activities, Portfolio Progress Reports, and the final chapter on preparing and presenting the portfolio. Current research and practice in language arts tells us the portfolio is not only an effective assessment device, but also a powerful instructional methodology, so we use it here. The portfolio embraces, rather than replaces, other elements of the book.

A third change is the addition of Speaker's Forum Projects. These are whole-class activities found at the end of sections. Each Forum Project is designed to bring together the main elements of a section into a public performance or presentation, a natural summing up activity for a speaking and listening book.

The five evaluation criteria students will use for their self-assessments can be used to describe this new edition of *Speaking by Doing*. Our purpose is to expand students' **range** and increase their **versatility**. Through their work they will understand the **connectedness** of their speaking and listening abilities to their personal, academic, and career goals. By developing **control** over their abilities and mastery of techniques, they will become more **independent** learners, as well as speakers and listeners.

A final change is to be found in Part Four, Supplemental Assessment Tools, in this *Teacher's Resource Book*. This part includes Chapter Checkup Questions which ask students to synthesize concepts in each chapter in some new way. These essay questions allow students to give individual responses that reveal the scope and sophistication of their understanding of chapter material. The questions also offer students additional practice in analyzing and organizing for written presentation.

SECTION REVIEW

The Preface sets up the book for students. It offers suggestions on how to use the text and complete the Activity Notebook, a key feature of the course. The Preface explains the purpose and importance both of speaking and listening, and of the portfolio approach the book takes to developing these language abilities.

Section 1 is designed to give students a comfortable and productive start. Besides gaining knowledge, they will be developing their abilities as effective communicators in a friendly and receptive atmosphere. The importance of these abilities is emphasized by their immediate connection to personal, course, and career goals. Students will complete a preliminary self-assessment and begin working toward the building of a portfolio of speaking and listening activities.

Chapter 1, "Introduction," discusses the importance of speaking and listening; it provides students with assignments that lead them to a personal investigation of the importance of speech in a democracy. Several of the assignments call for participation in class discussions.

Chapter 2, "The Nature and Purposes of Speech Communication," deals primarily with human communication as a process. The concept of process is presented and the factors of the process are enumerated and defined. The explanation makes clear that each factor is crucial—without each, there is no communication.

The important concepts of "self-talk," listening, feedback, noise, and channels are presented. If the course outline does not permit in-depth exploration of this chapter, the basic concepts should be introduced in other portions of the course.

Chapter 3, "Getting Acquainted in a New Community," has several goals. First, it explores the feelings of individuals living in a mobile society. This exploration is a prelearning consideration, preparing students for the last chapter of the section, which deals with speech apprehension. Chapter 3 also sets forth the importance of knowing the audience and having the audience know the speaker. Audience analysis and the role and importance of feedback are introduced. The concept of "breaking the ice" is presented. Along with addressing the problems of getting acquainted, assignments and activities deal with the courtesies and skills needed to make introductions in social settings.

Chapter 4, "Social Conversation," is an extension of Chapter 3. Its primary objective is to make students aware of the importance of feeling at ease in social settings. Students are introduced to an array of ideas relating to conversation, drawn from the minds of thinkers throughout the ages. Adequate practice in conversation and in analyzing feedback regarding students' contributions are provided.

Chapter 5, "Speech Fears and Self-Confidence," is probably one of the most important chapters in the text. Too many texts fail to deal significantly with this topic. The authors are convinced that until a person knows and understands the normalcy and value of human fear behaviors, he or she will never gain a healthy self-concept or learn to utilize fear positively.

Chapter 6, "Speech Communication and Your Future," discusses the importance of communication in the world. Career decision making continues to be of great concern to educators. The problems connected with any decision making are related to the thought processes and language use of the individual. Study after study demonstrates that speech skills—both speaking and listening—are central to getting, holding, and advancing in a job. Studies also have demonstrated that speech apprehension plays a major role in career development.

The current age is being called the communication age. Increasingly the world of industry is looking for people with competencies in human communication. Specific jobs now exist for "communication" personnel. Chapter 6 has been extensively revised in this edition to articulate more effectively with the rest of the text. The major speech skill all students will need is interviewing. This subject is dealt with at length.

In Section 2, students learn how to plan and prepare a speech—starting with a general topic and ending with specific ways to rehearse all aspects of the presentation.

Chapter 7, "Contexts, Audiences, Topics, and Purposes," deals with audiences and power relationships, the all-important speaking context. Several thinking and organizing frameworks are developed for presentation of different purposes.

"Writing for Success: Using the Tricks of the Trade," is Chapter 8. A "nuts and bolts" chapter, it is one of the central chapters of the book. It shows students how to select topics, analyze the audience, organize all features of the speech, use notes and use various types of language in developing style.

Chapters 9 to 12 extend the earlier parts of this section to using voice, using body language, and using support materials such as handouts and audio and visual aids, and speech rehearsal and evaluation techniques.

Section 3, "Oral Interpretation and Storytelling," begins the specialized sections of the book.

Chapter 13, "Oral Interpretation," concerns reading aloud to others for the purposes of entertainment and literary appreciation. It builds on the speech skills learned in earlier chapters. Effective oral interpretation requires skill in articulation, pronunciation, and voice. In addition, the oral interpreter needs to be able to make the feelings and ideas of the author seem real to the listener. This requires an understanding of human needs, empathy, and motivation.

Chapter 14, "Telling a Good Story," presents the importance of storytelling yesterday and today. It encourages students to learn the skills of storytelling and presents assignments leading to skill development.

Section 4, another specialized section, deals with speaking for information and demonstration. Chapter 15, "Defining and Locating Information," deals with the nature of information and the role it plays. It also gives students experience in finding and retrieving information from libraries and other resources. Chapters 16 and 17 specifically address the special needs of informational and demonstration presentations.

Section 5, "Speaking for Persuasion and Problem Solving," introduces students to the importance of speech in group problem solving. It introduces persuasion and discussion as the two major modes of resolving group problems.

Chapter 18, "Speaking to Persuade," presents the nature, role, uses, and values of persuasion and discussion. It provides activities in studying groups and group problems so that students can choose topics for persuasion that are real and current, and that touch others in the classroom. This study of important and real problems also forms a basis for the activities in Chapter 19, "Problem Solving in Groups."

Chapter 19 is an experiential chapter; it involves students in the analysis and exploration of real problems and offers direction and information that result in development of skills in democratic problem solving. The concept of critical thinking, introduced earlier, is explored in a series of group activities.

Chapter 20, dealing with parliamentary procedure, provides a tool for more formal group problem solving. Most students will have more involvement with groups that use parliamentary procedure than with groups that use consensus. This chapter should be useful to all students in school settings where clubs and student government use parliamentary law.

The last section, Section 6, "Preparing and Presenting Your Portfolio," consists of assignments designed for completing the summary self-assessment and preparing and presenting the Speaking and Listening Portfolio.

SUGGESTIONS FOR USING THE TEXT

This edition of *Speaking by Doing* is no different from preceding editions in its educational philosophy—it is designed to require a large degree of student involvement. In this new edition, students are instructed to create their own Activity Notebooks. You need to be aware of the central need for such a student Notebook.

Speaking by Doing is punctuated with "assignments." Each assignment is numbered and has a title. A purpose statement indicates the objectives of each assignment. In addition to the assignments, there are a number of Activities suggested at the ends of chapters. These are considered optional. Many of these require students to go beyond their classroom involvement to implement the skills they are developing.

The text assignments are of two types. In the first type, students respond to questions and ideas primarily for their own learning. These assignments should be entered in the Activity Notebook, and you will need to monitor their completion. In the second type of assignment, students participate in class discussion or in speech presentations. Becoming ready to participate in class depends on completing the first type of assignment.

You are encouraged to discuss the importance of the Activity Notebook on the first day of class. Work with your students to design a notebook that will satisfy your needs and theirs. Some guidelines for setting up the Activity Notebook are provided in the Preface to the student text. A uniform Activity Notebook will be helpful to both you and your students.

You are also encouraged to insist that the Activity Notebook is essential to the success of the student in the course work. If you conclude that certain assignments can be bypassed, inform the student. You need, of course, to follow your own needs and educational objectives.

The Activity Notebook is the storehouse of materials for the Speaking and Listening Portfolio, another new feature of this edition. If students are to be truly independent, they must be responsible for keeping—and keeping track of—their own work. If students are to produce and present a portfolio, they must have a wide range of their own work from which to choose. And if students are to manage their own lifelong development as speakers and listeners, they must learn to use such tools as the Activity Notebook for organizing and monitoring their own growth.

In this Teacher's Resource Book, you will find a number of Feedback Forms designed for you to give students following presentations. These can be duplicated, but, if they are, they should be the same size as the students' Activity Notebooks so they can be readily inserted. These Feedback Forms are designed to correlate with the feedback checklists found in the final assignments of many chapters.

In addition to the Feedback Forms, we have included a number of blank forms, surveys, self-inventories, and charts that students may find helpful for certain important assignments. Rather than have students make their own, you may find that for uniformity and class management it is helpful to duplicate these forms as well.

Please note the suggested study procedure in the Preface to the student text. We believe that one learns best when there is a logical approach to learning. You may wish to remind students of this study procedure each time you begin a new chapter. This may at first seem a useless redundancy; however, our experience with teenagers is that they need such reminding. A certain routine, repetition, and reminder can help students get in the right frame of mind for successful learning.

Each chapter begins with a Preview page that lists the learning goals treated in the chapter. You should review these goals with your students. This is a good time for you to make clear your own perceptions of the intent of the chapter. You may wish to add learning goals that are important to your students or to the community.

The Chapter Challenge that opens each chapter will help to focus attention on one of the summary or endpoint activities of the chapter. Each Challenge helps the student begin the questioning process required for active learning.

One of the key aspects of the study procedure is the request that students prepare questions as a result of reading the Preview and Summary pages. Encourage this behavior. Set aside time to deal with those questions before beginning the text and the assignments for the chapter. If there is one major weakness in today's education, it is the absence of attention to sustaining childhood curiosity and developing it into adolescence. Encouraging students to think and question will help them develop this important life skill.

If the students read the Preview and Summary pages and prepare questions that arise from this reading, they should be ready to begin the reading and the assignments. However, we also have prepared sets of true and false questions for each chapter. Although these may be used as quizzes for grading purposes, we suggest that they be used as learning motivations for students. Present the quizzes, or similar sets of questions, to students as they begin each chapter. Ask them to find the correct answers as they explore the chapter.

In designing a course of study, there are three other matters that deserve consideration. First, it is helpful to provide time so that certain speech assignments can be repeated. Students generally learn a great deal with a first experience of their own; even more might be learned from observing others doing essentially the same thing. To be able to repeat an assignment and demonstrate what has been learned is exceedingly satisfying to a self-concept. To be able to "do a better job next time" is part of the learning process and should not be overlooked.

Second, impromptu speaking is an important learning device. It is discussed in the text, and suggestions are made there for its incorporation in the course. For helpful suggestions on the role of extemporaneous speech, you may refer to National Textbook's forensic handbook *Creative Speaking*, 2nd Edition, by David A. Frank.

Third, effective and productive learning takes place when the course of study has a "current" that keeps students moving through the activities. The Speaking and Listening Portfolio is designed to produce this current. Each chapter ends with a Building Your Portfolio activity to update what has been learned, and each section ends with a Portfolio Progress Report to sum up development in information, competency, and work habits. Although some students see the portfolio as a carrot, while others see it as a stick, the point is that they all *see* it. If you emphasize the portfolio feature of this book, the course will always be heading somewhere, toward that final performance.

In the student text you will find lists of suggested speech topics. These are placed there for help; they are not intended to be the topics students must use. We are strong believers in the rights of individuals to choose their own topics. Only two limitations should be placed on topic selection: (1) the topic should be within the bounds of good taste, and (2) the topic should be safe, in the sense that no dangerous objects are brought to class.

We hope this revised edition of *Speaking by Doing* meets your needs and expectations. You will no doubt observe that we have attempted to place public speaking in the perspective of a living democracy. In addition, we have attempted to provide experiences in which the role of the group can be emphasized. Both concepts are urgently needed and useful for all young citizens.

CURRICULUM PLANNING

Time constraints are a reality in many curricula. Speech instruction too often is given less consideration than it deserves and is sandwiched into English or social studies classes. Planning a course devoted to speaking and listening can be problematic. Here are suggestions for course work, given various time structures.

Because the portfolio is such an important feature of this revised edition, it is recommended that you plan to include it in whatever time frame you work in.

A TWO-SEMESTER COURSE

Speaking by Doing has been created for a one-year, two-semester course for beginning students in public speaking. The text can be easily completed in that period, including time for repeating major assignments. There can be considerable modification of the use of the text to support special interests of the students and teacher. For example, if interest in storytelling, pantomime, or oral interpretation is high, students can spend more time in these areas and choose to bypass other aspects of the text. If students have a high interest in persuasion, group discussion, and parliamentary procedure, these sections can be expanded and performance assignments can be repeated.

Although Sections 1 and 2 should be completed in order, Sections 2 to 5 can be done in any order, depending on the needs of your course and students. Section 6, including the summary self-assessment and portfolio presentation, should be completed last.

There is no way to recommend how much time to spend on any one chapter or unit within a chapter. The number of students in elective courses—and most speech courses are elective—varies greatly. Your planning in terms of time must be related to your class size.

A ONE-SEMESTER COURSE

For a one-semester course, you might use all or parts of these chapters: 1 to 12, 15 and 16, 18, and 21. If students in the course are well acquainted and relate well, you might skip some chapters of the opening section.

A NINE-WEEK COURSE

If you have only nine to ten weeks for the course, you can do the basics with all or parts of these chapters: 1, 5 to 8, 11, 12, 15, 16, 18, and 21.

It is somewhat presumptuous to outline a course, regardless of the time constraints. Most teachers are aware of what they want, what they can do, and what their students need the most. The materials in *Speaking by Doing* have been used many ways. For example, individual chapters have been used in a public-speaking course for college freshmen.

LESSON PLANS

This new edition of *Speaking by Doing* is admirably suited for the teacher who needs to prepare lesson plans. The text is organized in units that need little modification to become lesson plans. The chapters furnish Learning Goals, the assignments parallel these goals, and each chapter is presented in a series of clearly organized steps.

LISTENING AS
PART OF SPEAKING

Speaking by Doing is a text not just for speakers but for listeners as well. Human communication always occurs between two or more people, and listening behaviors are as important as speaking behaviors.

The text deals with listening throughout its pages. Often, attention to listening takes the form of dealing with *feedback*. Feedback is the action of a listener that reveals his or her listening behavior; paying attention to feedback and stressing its role in the communication process strengthens students' understanding of the central role of listening in communication. Specific aspects of listening are also discussed in the text—empathy, critical listening, levels of meaning, and analyzing the needs of others.

Research on listening has indicated that listening skills can be learned. But research also indicates that the teaching of listening skills needs to be conscious and deliberate. Following are some important concepts regarding the function of listening and the importance of teaching listening skills.

Listening is a major mode of human learning. For some it is the dominant learning mode. Increasingly, television has replaced print as the primary source of information, and television is dominated by visual as opposed to verbal language. This shift is very likely making significant differences in the listening behaviors of students. When the brain is programmed with the predominantly visual, it becomes a silent system unless it finds verbal or oral means of externalizing itself. A course in speaking and listening can assist students in discovering that auditory input to the brain can have beneficial results.

Listening abilities are determined by the significance placed on listening by parents and by the amount of time given to listening to children. Children learn that listening is important only when they discover they are worthy of being heard.

Listening abilities, at any given time, also are determined by the physical, emotional, and mental condition of the listener. Low skills in listening at the high school level should alert the teacher to possibilities of problems in these three areas.

In all activity designed for teaching listening behaviors, the listener must have a reason for listening. Unless incoming messages are related in some way to individual needs, those messages are seldom heeded. Avoiding pain or seeking a reward are not the best reasons for listening.

Listening and thinking are virtually the same human process. Listening is the determination of the meaning of incoming stimuli. One does not learn to do that simply by being told, "Hey, you! Pay attention!" Listening requires that the receiver bring experiences associated with language to the message.

For teachers concerned about the listening skills of their students, we offer the following suggestions.

1. Whenever possible, arrange the physical environment so that speakers and listeners can see and hear one another. In class discussions, arrange the students in a circle so there is face-to-face communication.

2. Learning to listen occurs when there is a good model. Monitor your own listening behaviors and make an effort to "hear" what is being said. Give feedback to all so that each student senses his or her value and importance.

3. Listen not only to what is said but also to what is not said. Listening with a third ear and to hidden agendas are important when listening to the teenager.

4. Listen actively to build your own Speaking and Listening Portfolio. There is much to be learned about your own abilities by attending to what your classmates do well (and not so well).

STUDENT EVALUATION

Feedback is the process by which the receiver of a message tells the originator or sender that the message was received; in what condition the message seemed to be; what the message meant to the receiver; what changes in the receiver took place, or will take place; and perhaps what the sender should do or how to do it.

All feedback is a process of evaluation. Without feedback there is very little chance that a system will modify its behaviors. All feedback, however, does not originate outside the speaker. The speaker has the capacity to become a self-feedback system, a self-evaluator.

There is a very difficult problem with all evaluations: The person who gets the feedback (evaluation) invariably intentionalizes it. This means he or she cannot separate the evaluation of the message from the "goodness" of the self. It is almost a truth—"All evaluations hurt."

For young people, the problem of not being able to separate criticism of a message from criticism of the ego is particularly acute. The emerging ego in a rapidly changing body is at its most fragile stage. It is a rare teenager who clearly comprehends that evaluation does not always imply some form of personal rejection.

Feedback and evaluation, however, are inescapable in teaching effective communication. Whichever system of evaluation you choose, keep in mind the following:

1. All human egos are tender, tenuous, and finite.

2. Discuss fully the role of evaluation as essentially a corrective feedback process, and make students aware of evaluation criteria prior to the evaluation.

3. Discuss fully the problem of trying to separate evaluative feedback from an attack on the ego.

4. Make sure that all learning experiences are clearly defined so that students sense when evaluation is indeed constructive, connective feedback.

5. Do not tolerate feedback from students' peers that are personal attacks on the speaker.

6. Do not assume the role of being the only source of evaluative feedback. Keep in mind that all students in the class are listeners, all students are receiving messages, and all students need to participate in telling the speaker of their reactions to the received message.

7. Always involve the students in determining what they should be listening for.

8. Remember, no two people are the same or can occupy the same place at the same time. Therefore, no two listeners (including the teacher) will hear the same message. A speaker has the right to get feedback from all listeners.

9. Keep in mind that evaluation and feedback are *not* the same as grading. All grading is the making of value judgments. Never grade anyone or anything unless you are required to. All grading systems invariably attack or support the ego.

10. Finally, use the portfolio concept—that all students are involved in building their repertoires of information, competencies, and work habits—as a constant reminder that feedback is necessary for growth and development.

In planning a day's class or a unit, be sure to allow time for oral feedback. Studies in behavior modification demonstrate that (1) immediate feedback is more useful than delayed feedback, (2) positive feedback is more useful than negative feedback, and (3) no feedback will help eliminate undesirable behaviors more efficiently than will negative feedback.

When first allowed to participate in feedback as an evaluative process, students will tend to pick out negative behaviors. Allow students to spend the first several feedback sessions citing only positive reinforcements. Later, when negative feedback is included, have the positive feedback come first.

Feedback Forms can be found at the end of this Resource Book. You may duplicate them prior to each speech assignment and give them to the speaker following the speech activity. In the text there are listener's feedback checklists for students that are related to the Feedback Forms. You will want to discuss these checklists with your students.

There are many options for evaluating student work, assessing progress, and assigning grades. Although students often think these three activities are interchangeable, instructors have seen, for example, that the student who makes the most progress does not necessarily receive the highest grade for a course. And the student who gives the two best speeches of the year might not receive an "A" because of weaker work on other assignments.

Every instructor works in an institutional context that makes some prescription about assessment, evaluation, and grades. Further, every instructor has preferences based on experience, style, and the particular student he or she meets. Rather than prescribe an evaluation design, we will list the textbook features and suggest some purposes for which they might be used.

Activity Notebook: As the course proceeds, this becomes a developmental resource which gives instructor and student a look at the body of work produced. The Activity Notebook is also the basis for all Speaking and Listening Portfolio activities. Although we have suggested that the Activity Notebook be required, it can be a graded or ungraded requirement.

Chapter Assignments and Activities: These are the chief learning materials of the text. Opportunities for feedback and response are provided for many of these. Each assignment or activity can be graded separately, grades can be reserved for the larger tasks only, or the individual assignments can be ungraded until Progress Report or Portfolio Presentation time.

Suggested Additional Activities: Same as Chapter Assignments and Activities.

Chapter Checkup Questions: These can be given as a check on students' ability to synthesize chapter materals independently. Although the Checkup Questions could be used and graded as tests, they can also be used as ungraded assignments.

Speaker's Forum Projects: These are the end-of-section projects, which involve the most preparation time, the most "public" presentation, and the most feedback or response from classmates.

Building Your Portfolio Activities:	These lead directly into the Portfolio Progress Reports and, finally, the Portfolio Presentation.
Portfolio Progress Reports:	These are opportunities to reflectively analyze one's own work and progress in the course. Although the focus is not on grades, it is easy to modify these forms so as to include a grade proposal feature.
Preliminary and Summary Self-Assessments:	These are not meant to be graded activities. Rather, they provide individual "bench-marks" for students at the beginning and end of their work with the text. Growth and development are the issues.
Portfolio Presentation:	There is a rating form for response to this final presentation. It can be modified to include a suggested grade, or grading can be reserved for the instructor.

SUGGESTED
ADDITIONAL ACTIVITIES

Most chapters of *Speaking by Doing* contain a sufficient number of assignments. However, there may be a need for more or different exercises. For example, in Chapter 3, "Getting Acquainted in a New Community," you may want to select icebreaking activities that fit your particular teaching environment.

One or two additional activities can be found at the end of most chapters; for other chapters, even more activities are suggested. This section presents further possible activities for each chapter.

SECTION 1:   WHY WE SPEAK

1.   INTRODUCTION

1. Hold a class discussion on one or more of the following topics:
   a. What is a "feral" child? Do feral children develop mentally as do normal children? Do they develop language skills?
   b. How do they communicate? What happens to individual creativity in a dictatorship?
   c. What happens to language and thought when a person has a stroke affecting speech centers in the brain?

2. Ask each student to select one of the written assignments from Chapter 1 and share it with the class.

3. Have the class prepare a set of Learning Goals based on their responses in Assignment 1–3, "Why I Am Taking This Course." List these goals on a chart for display in the classroom.

2.   THE NATURE AND PURPOSES OF SPEECH COMMUNICATION

1. Discuss the following questions:
   a. How is a single human being a complete communication system?
   b. What roles do history, literature, mythology, family stories, and folktales play in the life of a culture?
   c. In what ways is communication the "glue" that holds societies together?
   d. How does the ability of the human being to build and use a language distinguish humans from other animal systems?

3.   GETTING ACQUAINTED IN A NEW COMMUNITY

1. Provide students with a list of "information" that must be discovered by talking with their classmates. Have the students move freely around the class, seeking out the information. When finished, the students can share their discoveries.

    Instructions to students: Your task is to find someone in your class who fits each of the following descriptions. Have the student who fits the description sign your list. Try to find a different person for each description; include your teacher as a resource.

    a. An only child

    b. Skipped breakfast today

    c. Drives a sports car

    d. Owns a motorcycle

    e. Owns a moped

    f. Doesn't get enough sleep

    g. Plays a musical instrument

    h. Is left-handed

    i. Is taller than you

    j. Has an unusual hobby

    k. Has visited a foreign country

    l. Works outside of school

    m. Writes poetry

    n. Has a dog

    o. Likes sailing

    p. Has the same favorite food as yours

    q. Hunts or fishes

    r. Speaks a language other than English

    s. Has performed in a play

    t. Plays a varsity sport

2. In a speech class everyone should know everyone else's name and how to pronounce it. Divide the class into dyads. Have each member of the dyad interview the other member, learning as much as possible that can be shared with the class. Students can use their Personal Inventories (Assignment 3–3) as a guide for conducting the interview.

    Next, have each student introduce his or her partner in the following manner. The first person introduces the partner to the class by stating and spelling the partner's first and last names and giving some information about the partner. The partner then reciprocates.

    After the second person speaks, he or she chooses a third person, who introduces his or her partner. This time, however, the third person introduces his or her partner only to the first two people. The first and last names of all three people being introduced are said aloud. In turn, the partner (fourth person) introduces the third person. Again, the person who speaks last chooses a fifth person, who introduces his or her partner to the four previously introduced persons, giving the first and last names of both the person being introduced and the four to whom the person is being introduced. Proceed in this manner until all the partners in the class have introduced each other.

3. Arrange students in a circle. One student begins by saying his or her first name along with a descriptive word that begins with the same letter as the name. (Examples: "My name is Angela, but I'm no angel." "My name is David and I like to dance.") Each student that follows gives the name and description of all the preceding persons.

4. Arrange students in a circle. Have each student say his or her name and then complete such phrases as

   a. "I feel_____."

   b. "I think that _____."

   c. "I wish that _____."

   d. "I dreamed that _____."

   e. "I plan to _____."

5. For the first two weeks of school, or until students are well acquainted, have students sit in different places each class session. Encourage them to take time to get acquainted.

6. Ask students to make collages or find pictures or objects that represent some aspect of themselves and to present these to the class. Classmates are encouraged to ask questions or make (positive) comments.

4. SOCIAL CONVERSATION

1. Divide the class into conversation groups. Place a number of topics for conversation in a box or hat and have each group select a topic for an impromptu conversation. Videotape each group and play back the tape for commentary from the class.

2. Have a group of three students present a conversation on a topic that you choose. Remind each student to not let others steal the topic and run away with it. However, before the presentation, assign one of the participants to be a "topic thief" and to do everything possible to steal the subject and dominate the conversation. After the activity, discuss the reactions of the participants and the class.

5. SPEECH FEARS AND SELF-CONFIDENCE

The activities for Chapter 5 are arranged according to the list on page 54 of the student text, "Five Facts about Fear and Self-Confidence."

1. *All normal people experience fear when they are faced with tasks that really matter.*

   • Have students interview adults in the community. Let them use the Fear Inventory (Assignment 5–2) as the basis for their interviews. For example, interview athletic coaches, trial lawyers, union leaders, politicians, parents, relatives, and so forth. Have students report their findings.

- Have a small group of students prepare and send a questionnaire based on the Fear Inventory (Assignment 5–2) to famous individuals, such as astronauts, musicians, sports champions, or movie stars. Have them report their findings. Be sure an explanatory cover letter accompanies the questionnaire.

- If possible, invite a mental health professional to speak to the class on the subject of "The Normalcy and Meaning of Emoting." For this activity, send the invited guest a copy of all the items appearing on page 54 under the heading, "Five Facts about Fear and Self-Confidence." Be sure to leave plenty of time for questions and discussion. If a psychiatrist is not available, invite another qualified person, such as a religious leader, counselor, medical doctor, or speech/debate team coach.

2. *Fear is useful and desirable when understood, but it is wasteful and undesirable when misunderstood.*

   - Have a class discussion on the meaning of the word *misunderstood*. Have students explore the consequences of misunderstood messages. Encourage them to cite personal examples.

   - Have a discussion on these questions: What is lying? Why do people lie? What are the results of lying? How does lying affect message making?

   - Hold class debates on the following propositions.

     a. Honesty is the best policy.

     b. Cowardice is never a wise behavior.

     c. Fear of being afraid is a waste of energy.

     d. Worry wastes more energy than war does.

   - Hold a class discussion on the role that pain plays in keeping us alive.

     a. What is pain?

     b. What role does it play in communication—intrapersonally and interpersonally?

     c. Why are headaches (the ability to have a headache) desirable?

     d. How can we come to accept the normalcy of pain?

     e. What is painful when fear is functioning?

   - Hold a class discussion on the question, "Can you be afraid if you are not being threatened?"

   - Invite a physics teacher (or other qualified science teacher) to class to discuss the principles of energy and relate them to emoting. Ask the visiting teacher to discuss workload, action-reaction, forms of energy, entropy, and homeostasis.

3. *All physical fear reactions have logical explanations.*

   - Invite a biology teacher to class to discuss the physiology of emoting. When you invite him or her, include a copy of the six questions in Assignment 5–7.

   - Hold a class debate or discussion on the question, "Can a normal person go through a 24-hour day and not experience some fear?"

- Discuss the question, "If blushing is normal, why are people 'ashamed' of blushing?" (Or, more generally, if fear is normal, why are humans afraid of admitting their fear?)
- Arrange a demonstration of a biofeedback machine or a lie detector. Invite a doctor, therapist, or law enforcement expert to talk to your class about such devices.

4. *All public appearance situations are situations that really matter.*
   - Ask students to share with the class the self-concept that, to them, is the most endangered during a speech.
   - Hold class discussions on the following questions:
     a. Why is it that although all people have fear, not all people fear the same thing?
     b. Are there relationships between what a person fears and the person's age, sex, family, race, national or cultural origin, or religion?
     c. How can a person get rid of a conditioned fear behavior when he or she learns that there is no danger in the stimulus?

5. *All self-confidence comes from experience.*
   - Discuss the real meaning of the following expressions:
     a. Take it one step at a time.
     b. Practice makes perfect.
     c. Nothing succeeds like success.
     d. Experience counts.
   - Have each student prepare two lists titled "I am confident about . . ." and "I am not confident about . . ." Have students discuss their lists in class.
   - You may want to share experiences when you were fearful or confident.

6.   SPEECH COMMUNICATION AND YOUR FUTURE

1. Set up several role-playing situations in which students have an opportunity to practice all the kinds of questions described in the chapter, that is, open-ended, telling back, yes or no, and so forth. These situations can be organized in pairs or groups of four. In the foursome, one person can ask a question, a second can answer it, and the other two, acting as observers, can provide alternative responses. Then, have students switch roles.

2. Have students select one of the careers mentioned in the chapter. Have the students research, prepare, and present a report on the training or education required, the job description, and the importance of communication in this career selection. Reports can be either written or oral.

SECTION 2:   PREPARING AND PRESENTING

7.   CONTEXTS, AUDIENCES, TOPICS, AND PURPOSES

1. Hold a discussion about the meaning of *brainstorming*. Conduct a brainstorming session for "finding a better way." Divide the class into four work groups. Give each group the same problem to solve and instruct them to do it by brainstorming. Suggested problems might be "How to make a better pencil," "How to improve traffic flow around the school," or "How to improve the speech textbook."

2. Ask a member of the science faculty to address the class on the subject of orderliness in scientific thinking. Inform the speaker that you are studying organization of data.

8.   WRITING FOR SUCCESS: USING THE TRICKS OF THE TRADE

1. Ask each student to prepare a character sketch of a very good friend or a famous person. Have students give special attention to the use of adjectives and adverbs, and ask each student to read his or her sketch in class.

2. Have students pretend they are reporters writing about an experience they have had. Ask them to describe the experience as strongly as they can.

3. Ask your students to read a newspaper editorial and a news article. Have them identify differences in writing styles. Ask them to read a novel or short story and compare the style with that of a "how-to" book.

9.   YOUR VOICE AND ITS POWERS

1. Divide the class into four listening groups. Have each group listen to the evening news on at least three networks and rank the newscasters for their voice quality. Have students discuss their rankings in class.

2. Invite a singer (a school staff member, a soloist, or a local choral director) to class to discuss the importance of breathing to the singing process. Also ask him or her to discuss the importance of "educating" the voice.

3. Record each student reading the same passage of prose or poetry. Play back the voices and ask the class to match the voice with the person; ask students to pick out the voices that sound the best and to explain their choices.

10.   USING BODY LANGUAGE

1. Show a film or tape of a pantomime or a movie featuring Charlie Chaplin, Ned Sparks, Jimmy Durante, or Laurel and Hardy. Discuss the importance of body language in these productions.

2. Have students bring to class pictures taken from magazines that they think reveal certain types of feelings or moods; share them and discuss them.

3. Play a game of charades. Have students bring topics for the game. Divide the class into two groups and play three rounds; the winners get a treat from the losers. This is a very effective method for getting students loosened up and free to use gestures.

11.   USING SUPPORT MATERIALS

1. Divide the class into four production units and assign each unit to make a ten-minute video. Students can make an advertisement, a safety tape, an antidrug tape, a physical fitness tape, and so forth. Sound support for the tapes should be used.

2. Invite the drama teacher to class to discuss lighting, sound, music, makeup, sets, and costumes as forms of nonverbal communication.

3. Invite local television, advertising, or public relations experts to class to discuss the importance of nonverbal materials in producing effective results.

4. Divide the class into groups. Each group is to prepare a play no longer than three minutes using only sounds; no verbal language may be used. Record these, if possible, or produce them over a school intercom.

12.   REHEARSING AND MONITORING FOR SUCCESS

1. Invite a professional speaker to come in and explain how he or she rehearses (or helps others rehearse) for a presentation. The speaker might be a media announcer, a lawyer, a debate coach, a priest or minister, an actor or actress, etc.

2. Ask for some volunteers from the class to have Plan B tested. For these volunteers, create a problem—the power goes off for the slide projector, the microphone stops working, etc.—that requires them to switch to Plan B.

SECTION 3:   ORAL INTERPRETATION AND STORYTELLING

13.   ORAL INTERPRETATION

1. Encourage multicultural studies and the discussion of cultural differences, particularly in terms of literature performed in oral interpretation.

2. Ask students to write their own poetry or short story and read it to the class. Poetry is an attempt to externalize feelings that are often very personal and private. Teenagers in particular find such an activity valuable.

3. You may have students in class that do unusually well in oral interpretation; encourage them to participate in the forensic program if your school has one.

14.   TELLING A GOOD STORY

1. Have each student create a monstrous lie and then tell it to the class; have students rank the lies and select the best class liar.

SECTION 4:   SPEAKING FOR INFORMATION AND DEMONSTRATION

15.   DEFINING AND LOCATING INFORMATION

1. Invite local television and newspaper reporters to class to discuss their procedures for finding information.

2. Invite a lawyer or judge to class to discuss the meaning of *fact, opinion, evidence, proof,* and *argument.*

3. Give the class a list of facts that they must locate and verify. Students must have at least two different sources reporting the same fact. For variety, divide the class into small groups of three to five students and offer a reward for the group finding the most verified facts in the shortest time.

16.   PRESENTING THE SPEECH TO INFORM

1. Videotape the students when they practice polarizing so they can see themselves as others see them.

2. For this and all remaining chapters, hold a round of impromptu speeches. Put the emphasis on those speech communication objectives and major ideas that were dealt with in the chapter. Don't grade these speeches; emphasize fun and constructive feedback.

17.   THE DEMONSTRATION SPEECH

1. Secure a videotape of a demonstration, such as cooking, golf, or exercise. Play the tape for the class and discuss the techniques used by the demonstrator.

2. Humor can come from a "messed up" demonstration. Invite one or two of your "class comedians" to put on a demonstration for pure entertainment. Afterwards discuss why it was funny.

3. Ask each student to prepare an introduction for a well-known individual. Specify the type of audience, the day and time, and the purpose for the speech. Have students provide feedback on the power, accuracy, and impact of each introduction.

SECTION 5:   SPEAKING FOR PERSUASION AND PROBLEM SOLVING

18.   SPEAKING TO PERSUADE

1. One of the most effective ways to get young people to understand motivational language is to have them listen to and analyze TV, radio, and newspaper advertising. Have students listen to or read such persuasion and then prepare their own one-minute spot. When each is finished, the class should identify the motivation used and discuss the techniques of language used.

2. Tape several commercials and listen to them in class. Have students analyze each commercial for faulty logic, lack of evidence, and appeals to emotions that are unrelated to the object of the ad.

19.   PROBLEM SOLVING IN GROUPS

1. Before beginning the chapter, have students prepare a list of groups that they believe would use group problem solving. This list could include boards of directors, political bodies, fund-raising groups, boards of education, and so forth.

20.   PARLIAMENTARY PROCEDURE

1. Invite a parliamentarian to class to talk about the nature and the uses of parliamentary law.

2. At the end of the unit, hold a parliamentary procedure workshop in your school for leaders of all the classes, clubs, and organizations. Use your students as workshop leaders.

3. Have your class prepare a brief summary of the important rules and procedures; duplicate this and distribute it to all school leaders responsible for meetings.

SECTION 6:   PREPARING AND PRESENTING YOUR PORTFOLIO

1. Videotape the Portfolio Presentations for discussion or for inclusion in individual students' portfolios.

2. Make an instructional videotape for next year's class. During the weeks that portfolios are being prepared and presented, tape a panel discussion of five to eight classmates talking about requirements, problems, and ways of working out solutions to the demands of the Portfolio Presentation.

Part Two
Professional Resources

BOOKS AND ARTICLES ON TEACHING SPEECH COMMUNICATION

Allen, R. R., Kenneth Brown, and Joanne Yatvin. *Learning Language Through Communication: A Functional Approach.* Belmont, CA: Wadsworth, 1986.

Allen, R. R., S. Clay Willmington, and Jo Sprague. *Communication in the Secondary School: A Pedagogy.* 3d ed. Scottsdale, AZ: Gorsuch Scarisbrick, 1990.

Barker, Larry, ed. *Communication in the Classroom.* Englewood Cliffs, NJ: Prentice-Hall, 1982.

Bassett, Ronald, and Mary Boone. "Improving Speech Communication Skills: An Overview of the Literature." In Rebecca Rubin, ed. *Improving Speaking and Listening Skills.* San Francisco: Jossey, Bass, 1983, pp. 83–93.

Bock, Douglas G., and E. Hope Bock. *Evaluating Classroom Speaking.* Urbana, IL: ERIC and Speech Communication Association, 1981.

Boileau, Don. "Speaking/Listening; Much Used, Little Taught." *NASSP Curriculum Report.* Reston, VA: National Association of Secondary School Principals, 14 (December 1984).

Book, Cassandra, and Kathleen Galvin. *Instruction in and about Small Group Discussion.* Urbana, IL: ERIC and Speech Communication Association, 1975.

Callahan, Joseph, and Leonard Clark. *Teaching in the Middle and Secondary Schools: Planning for Competence.* New York: Macmillan, 1982.

Civikly, Jean. *Classroom Communication.* Dubuque, IA: William C. Brown, 1992.

Classroom Activities in Speaking and Listening. Madison, WI: Wisconsin Department of Public Instruction, 1991.

Cooper, Pamela J., ed. *Activities for Teaching Speaking and Listening in Grades 7–12.* Annandale, VA: Speech Communication Association, 1985.

Cooper, Pamela J. *Speech Communication for the Classroom Teacher.* 4th ed. Scottsdale, AZ: Gorsuch Scarisbrick, 1991.

Cooper, Pamela J., and Kathleen Galvin. *Improving Classroom Communication.* Washington, DC: Dingle Associates, 1982.

DeFabio, Roseanne V. *Outcomes in Process: Setting Standards for Language Use.* Portsmouth, NH: Boynton/Cook Heinemann, 1994.

Frank, David A. *Creative Speaking.* 2d ed. Lincolnwood, IL: National Textbook Co., 1995.

Friedman, Paul. *Communicating in Conferences: Parent-Teacher-Student Interaction.* Urbana, IL: ERIC and Speech Communication Association, 1980.

Gallo, Donald R. *Books for You.* Urbana, IL: National Council of Teachers of English, 1985.

Galvin, Kathleen, and Bernard Brommel. *Family Communication: Cohesion and Change.* 3d ed. New York: HarperCollins, 1991.

Gudykunst, William, and Young Yun Kim. *Communicating with Strangers: An Approach to Intercultural Communication.* 2d ed. New York: McGraw-Hill, 1992.

Hawley, Robert C., and Isabel Hawley. *Human Values in the Classroom: A Handbook for Teachers.* New York: Hart, 1975.

Hays, Ellis R. *Interact: Communication Activities for Personal Life Strategies.* San Francisco: International Society for General Semantics, 1974.

Hetherington, M. Sue. "The Importance of Oral Communication." *College English,* 44 (October 1982): 570–574.

Holbrook, Hilary Taylor. "Oral Language: A Neglected Language Art?" *Language Arts,* 60 (February 1983): 255–258.

Jensen, J. Vernon. "Oral Skills Enhance Learning." *Improving College and University Teaching,* 28 (Spring 1980): 78–80.

Johnson, Eric. *Teaching School: Points Picked Up.* New York: Walker and Co., 1981.

Klopf, Donald W. *Intercultural Encounters: The Fundamentals of Intercultural Communication.* Englewood, CO: Morton, 1987.

Larson, Carl E. "Problems in Assessing Functional Communication." *Communication Education,* 27 (November 1978): 304–309.

Littlejohn, S. *Theories of Human Communication.* 4th ed. Belmont, CA: Wadsworth, 1992.

Lounsbury, John H. "As I See It: The Most Neglected (and Important?) Basic." *Middle School Journal,* XV (August 1984): 2.

May, Frank B. *To Help Children Communicate.* Columbus, OH: Charles Merrill, 1980.

Purves, Alan, Joseph Quattrini, and Christine Sullivan. *Creating the Writing Portfolio.* Lincolnwood, IL: National Textbook Company, 1995.

Quattrini, Joseph A. *Successful Business Presentations.* Blue Ridge Summit, PA: TAB Books, 1990.

Rubin, Don, and Nancy Mead. *Large Scale Assessment of Oral Communication Skills K–12.* Urbana, IL: ERIC, 1984.

Samovar, Larry, and Richard Porter. *Intercultural Communication.* 6th ed. Belmont, CA: Wadsworth, 1991.

Seiler, William, L. David Schuelke, and Barbara Lieb-Brilhart. *Communication for the Contemporary Classroom.* New York: Holt, Rinehart, and Winston, 1984.

Sharan, Shlomo, and Yael Sharan. *Small Group Teaching.* Englewood Cliffs, NJ: Educational Technology Publications, 1976.

Simon, Sidney B., Leland W. Howe, and Howard Kirschenbaum. *Values Clarification: A Handbook for Teachers and Students.* New York: Hart, 1972.

Speech Communication Teacher. A quarterly journal of speech activities available from the Speech Communication Association, 5105 Backlick Road, Bldg. #E, Annandale, VA 22003.

Stewart, Lea, Alan Stewart, Sheryl Friedley, and Pamela Cooper. *Communication Between the Sexes.* 2d ed. Scottsdale, AZ: Gorsuch Scarisbrick, 1990.

Tannen, Deborah. *You Just Don't Understand: Women and Men in Conversation.* New York: Ballantine, 1990.

Thaiss, Christopher, and Charles Suhor, eds. *Speaking and Writing K–12.* Urbana, IL: National Council of Teachers of English, 1984.

Wood, Barbara. *Children and Communication.* 2d ed. Englewood Cliffs, NJ: Prentice-Hall, 1981.

Wood, Barbara, ed. *Development of Functional Communication Skills: Grades 7–12.* Urbana, IL: ERIC and Speech Communication Association, 1977.

PROFESSIONAL ASSOCIATIONS

American Forensic Association, c/o James Pratt, Executive Secretary, University of Wisconsin–River Falls, River Falls, WI 54022.

American Speech and Hearing Association, 10801 Rockville Pike, Rockville, MD 20852.

International Communication Association, Balcones Research Center, 10100 Burnet Road, Austin, TX 78758.

International Listening Association, 366 North Prior Avenue, St. Paul, MN 55104.

National Association for the Preservation and Perpetuation of Storytelling, P.O. Box 309, Jonesborough, TN 37699.

National Catholic Forensic League, c/o Richard P. Gaudette, Secretary/Treasurer, 21 Nancy Road, Milford, MA 01757.

National Council of Teachers of English, 1111 Kenyon Road, Urbana, IL 61801.

National Forensic League, P.O. Box 38, Ripon, WI 54971.

Speech Communication Association, 5105 Backlick Road, Bldg. #E, Annandale, VA 22003.

Part Three
Blackline Masters

FEEDBACK FORMS

This section contains Feedback Forms for use with speaking assignments. These forms help listeners to create listening agendas, and also help speakers to understand the effects and the effectiveness of their work. These forms can be duplicated for classroom use and may be modified as needed to suit your particular class needs.

Some of the forms are designed for specific assignments, while others are more general forms suited to types of presentations or any presentation. In Sections 2 to 4, you might want to use more than one form—one for general commentary and another for specific techniques featured in that presentation.

Feedback is necessary for learning, but it is important that feedback begin in a safe and positive way. The speaking and listening activities in the early chapters are intended to create an atmosphere in which students can develop a sense of acceptance, respect, and security. Feedback is most effective when it occurs constructively, without damaging the atmosphere of trust in the classroom community.

FEEDBACK FORM NO. 1

This general feedback form can be used with any presentation.

FEEDBACK FORM NO. 2

This form is to be used in connection with any speech or report to evaluate both speaking and listening skills. Some instructors use this form for each presentation done during the course.

FEEDBACK FORM NO. 3

This form is to be used with the speeches in Chapter 8, "Writing for Success: Using the Tricks of the Trade." It can be used in conjunction with Feedback Form No. 5.

FEEDBACK FORM NO. 4

This form is used in connection with the voice-only speeches in Chapter 9, "Your Voice and Its Powers." It can also be used in conjunction with Form No. 5.

FEEDBACK FORM NO. 5

This form is to be used for the nonverbal behavior speech in Chapter 10, "Using Body Language." It can also be used for any presentation where body language is featured.

FEEDBACK FORM NO. 6

This form is to be used with the audiovisual aids speeches in Chapter 11. It can be used with any speech where support materials are featured.

FEEDBACK FORM NO. 7

This form is to be used in connection with the presentation in Chapter 13, "Oral Interpretation."

FEEDBACK FORM NO. 8

This form is to be used with the storytelling assignments in Chapter 14, "Telling a Good Story."

FEEDBACK FORM NO. 9

This form is for use with the informative speech presentations in Chapter 16, "Presenting the Speech to Inform."

FEEDBACK FORM NO. 10

This form is for use with the demonstration speeches in Chapter 17.

FEEDBACK FORM NO. 11

This form is to be used with the persuasive speech assignment in Chapter 18, but it may also be useful for other speeches given during the course.

FEEDBACK FORM NO. 12

This form is to be used in connection with the major assignments in Chapter 19, "Problem Solving in Groups."

FEEDBACK FORM NO. 13

This is to be used with the Speaker's Forum Project (Portfolio Presentation) in Section 6.

Feedback Form No. 1

Name of Student _____ **Date** _____

Title of Speech _____

A. Introduction _____

_____

_____

_____

_____

_____

B. Main body of speech or report _____

_____

_____

_____

_____

_____

C. Conclusions _____

_____

_____

_____

_____

_____

D. Delivery _____

_____

_____

_____

_____

 (continued)

E. Language _____

_____

_____

_____

F. Bodily action _____

_____

_____

_____

G. Audience adaptation _____

_____

_____

_____

H. Voice _____

_____

_____

I. Rate _____

_____

_____

J. Fluency _____

_____

_____

_____

Feedback Form No. 2

Listener's Name _____ **Date** _____

Speaker's Name _____

Title of Speech _____

A. In the diagram below, check the circle that represents the degree to which you felt immersed or involved in the ideas, thinking, and feelings of the speaker.

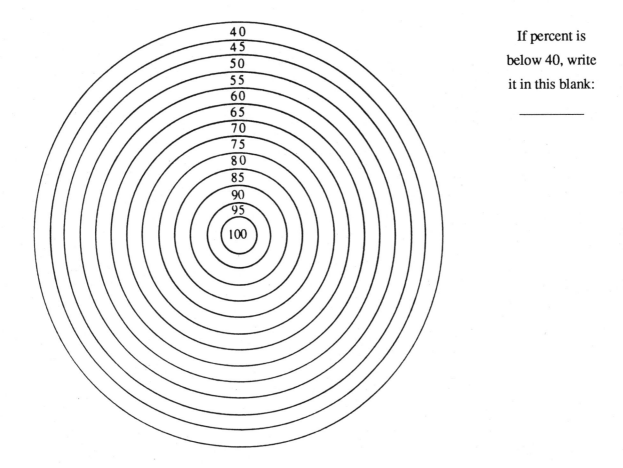

If percent is
below 40, write
it in this blank:

_____

B. In my judgment, the main point of this speech was _____

_____

_____

Feedback Form No. 3

Speaker's Name _____ Date _____

Title of Speech _____

A. Use of audience-contact language _____

_____

B. Did speaker have adequate basic statements? _____

_____

_____

C. Was there more descriptive language than usual for this speaker? _____

_____

_____

D. Was the descriptive language effective? Appropriate? Vivid? Real? _____

_____

_____

E. Was the action language adequate? _____

_____

_____

F. Did the speaker use good motivational language? _____

_____

_____

G. How effective was the bodily action? _____

_____

_____

H. If speaker used notes, were they effective? _____

_____

_____

Feedback Form No. 4

Speaker's Name _____ Date _____

Title of Speech _____

A. Breath control _____

B. Articulation

   1. Dropping final sounds _____

   2. Dropping medial sounds _____

   3. Substitutions _____

   4. Running sounds together _____

C. Volume

   1. Too soft _____

   2. Too loud _____

D. Projection

   1. Adequate _____

   2. Inadequate _____

E. Inflection

   1. Mistakes _____

   2. Good points _____

F. Emphasis

   1. Adequate _____

   2. Inadequate _____

G. Pronunciation

   1. Mistakes _____

   2. Good points _____

Feedback Form No. 5

Name of Speaker _____ **Date** _____

Title of Speech _____

Following are seven general items that affect nonverbal communication; after each item are a number of factors related to that item. Place a check mark beside each factor that best describes the nonverbal communication behavior of the speaker.

A. General attitude toward the audience

Alert _____

Enthusiastic _____

Communicative _____

Friendly _____

Personable _____

Retiring _____

Indifferent _____

Overaggressive _____

B. Dress

Appropriate _____

Neat _____

Not distracting _____

Careless _____

Inappropriate _____

Distracting _____

C. Posture

Erect _____

Poised _____

Balanced _____

Stiff _____

Body Sways _____

Unbalanced _____

D. Platform movement

Purposeful _____

Sufficient _____

Pacing _____

Shifting _____

None _____

E. Use of arms and hands

Natural _____

Meaningful _____

Well timed _____

Jerky _____

Cramped _____

Distracting _____

None _____

F. Facial expressions

Responsive _____

Animated _____

Pleasant _____

Exaggerated _____

Strained _____

Rigid _____

G. Eye contact _____

Direct _____

Sees everyone _____

Shifting _____

Avoiding _____

Sees only a few _____

Feedback Form No. 6

Name _____ Date _____

Title of Speech _____

A. Were the aids useful? _____

B. Were they well planned? _____

C. Were they well handled? _____

D. Could they be seen plainly by all? _____

E. Were they appropriate? _____

F. Did they support the main idea or did they dominate it? _____

_____

G. Was the speaker tied to the aids? _____

H. Did eye contact and audience contact suffer from the use of the aids? _____

_____

I. Did the speaker get good audience reaction? _____

J. Did the speaker receive feedback? _____

K. Summary _____

_____

_____

_____

_____

_____

Feedback Form No. 7

Reader's Name _____ Date _____

Type of Selection _____ Author _____

Title _____

A. Introduction _____

_____

_____

B. Reader's understanding of selection _____

_____

C. Vocal interpretation _____

_____

D. Bodily action and platform behavior _____

_____

E. Literary values of selection _____

_____

F. Suggestions for improvements

   1. Delivery _____

_____

_____

_____

_____

   2. Choice of materials _____

_____

_____

_____

_____

Feedback Form No. 8

Storyteller's Name _____ **Date** _____

Title _____

Author (if there was one) _____

A. **Introduction**

   1. **Was mood set?** _____

   2. **Was locale set?** _____

   3. **Was scene set?** _____

   4. **Were characters clear?** _____

B. **Story**

   1. **Was it appropriate?** _____

   2. **Did it seem true? believable?** _____

   3. **Was story well told?** _____

      a. **Use of language?** _____

      b. **Use of body and gestures?** _____

      c. **Use of voice?** _____

   4. **Was story concise, tight, held together?** _____

     _____

   5. **Was it fresh, new, entertaining?** _____

     _____

C. **Additional comments** _____

_____

_____

_____

_____

_____

Feedback Form No. 9

Name of Speaker _____ **Date** _____

Title of Speech _____

Speaker's Specific Purpose _____

A. **Purpose:** Was it clear? Was it accomplished? _____

_____

_____

_____

_____

B. **Introduction:** Was purpose clearly stated? Were listeners motivated? _____

_____

_____

_____

_____

C. **Body of speech:** Was organization clear? Was it followed? Was new and useful information presented?

_____

_____

_____

_____

D. **Conclusion:** Was information summarized? Were values of information reviewed? Was there a strong closing statement?

_____

_____

_____

_____

E. Delivery: Was it informal? Pleasant? Readily heard and understood? Was bodily action useful? Eye contact?

_____

_____

_____

_____

Feedback Form No. 10

Name of Speaker _____ **Date** _____

Title of Speech _____

Specific Purpose of Speech _____

A. **Statement of purpose** _____

_____

_____

B. **Title of speech** _____

_____

_____

C. **Apparent degree of speaker's effort** _____

_____

_____

D. **Introduction**

   1. **Attention devices used** _____

   2. **Motivation of audience** _____

   3. **Clarity of verbatim introduction** _____

E. **Body**

   1. **Was organizational method followed?** _____

   2. **Was information readily understood?** _____

   3. **Was information related to needs of audience?** _____

F. **Conclusion**

   1. **Was summary brief?** _____

   2. **Were importance and value of speech reviewed?** _____

   3. **Did speaker close with snappy, forceful punch line?** _____

G. The presentation

　1. Appearance _____

　2. Audience eye contact _____

　3. Handling of objects _____

　4. Use of language _____

H. Summary _____

_____

_____

_____

_____

_____

_____

_____

_____

_____

_____

Feedback Form No. 11

Name_____ Date _____

Title of Speech _____

Audience Intended _____

Circle W for weak; A for average; G for good; E for excellent.

A. **Speaker's thought and organization**

		W	A	G	E
1.	Subject Matter	W	A	G	E
2.	Personal knowledge	W	A	G	E
3.	Personal interest	W	A	G	E
4.	Audience concern	W	A	G	E
5.	Introduction	W	A	G	E
6.	Motivation	W	A	G	E
7.	Organization	W	A	G	E
8.	Solution	W	A	G	E
9.	Conclusion	W	A	G	E

B. **Language**

		W	A	G	E
1.	Vividness	W	A	G	E
2.	Appropriateness	W	A	G	E
3.	Suitability to topic	W	A	G	E
4.	Fluency	W	A	G	E
5.	Oral grammar	W	A	G	E
6.	Adjective use	W	A	G	E
7.	Audience contact	W	A	G	E
8.	Pronunciation	W	A	G	E

(continued)

C. Voice

    1. Inflection   W   A   G   E

    2. Stress   W   A   G   E

    3. Variety   W   A   G   E

    4. Volume   W   A   G   E

    5. Articulation   W   A   G   E

D. Bodily Action

    1. Poise   W   A   G   E

    2. Dress   W   A   G   E

    3. Posture   W   A   G   E

    4. Gestures   W   A   G   E

    5. Movements   W   A   G   E

    6. Eye Contact   W   A   G   E

Feedback Form No. 12

Participant's Name _____ Date _____

Problem Discussed _____

Type of discussion being used (panel, roundtable, brainstorming)

Use W for weak; A for average; G for good; E for excellent.

A. Participant was:

   1. Constructive _____   6. Self-controlled _____

   2. Courteously aggressive _____   7. Friendly _____

   3. Brief _____   8. Sincere _____

   4. Pertinent _____   9. Patient _____

   5. Adaptive _____ 10. A wise compromiser _____

B. Comments on relationships in group:

   1. Speaker listening to others _____

   2. Speaker supporting others _____

   3. Speaker demonstrating leadership behaviors _____

C. Other comments: _____

_____

_____

_____

_____

Feedback Form No. 13

Participant's Name _____ **Date** _____

Portfolio Presentation _____

Depth of Insight: the range and depth of understanding the student reveals about his or her own language abilities—includes connectedness to goals, precision of language, focus on performance, use of evaluation criteria, scope of the assessment, specific nature of claims.

Rating: 1   2   3   4   5   6

Comment: _____

_____

_____

Strength of Evidence: the quantity, power, and relevance of the evidence supporting the claims of growth and achievement, as well as the strength of the warrants that connect data to claims.

Rating: 1   2   3   4   5   6

Comment: _____

_____

_____

Elaboration and Completeness: the degree of detail and explanation of the case; the extent to which the case is *proven* rather than *stated*, or *shown* rather than merely *told*.

Rating: 1   2   3   4   5   6

Comment: _____

_____

_____

Clarity of Expression: the fluency with which the student can present a case—involves organization, diction, sentence structure, transitions, other elements of style, and elements of spoken presentation.

Rating: 1   2   3   4   5   6

Comment: _____

_____

_____

Overall Rating: _____

UTILITY FORMS

Certain assignments in the text require students to prepare and enter into their Activity Notebooks an extensive form, a set of responses, or some kind of inventory or survey. The forms in this section can be duplicated to assure uniformity of the students' responses, if such uniformity is desired. Brief descriptions of each form are listed here; the forms themselves appear on the following pages.

PERSONAL INVENTORY

To be used in connection with Assignment 3–3, "Know Thyself: The Personal Inventory." The Personal Inventory forms the basis for a number of important assignments, including making introductions, selecting topics for speeches, and preparing audience analyses. Students are referred to their Personal Inventories repeatedly in the text.

FEAR INVENTORY

To be used in connection with Assignment 5–2, "Fear Inventory." The Fear Inventory helps students understand that fear is a normal behavior. It also provides data for presenting a speech and for understanding that all people have important similarities and differences.

CHARACTERISTICS OF SUCCESS

To be used in connection with Assignment 6–1, "Your Definition of Success." Students are instructed to rank their characteristics of success in order to identify their career "satisfiers." While students are given direction in the text about organizing and ranking characteristics, use of this form may provide less confusion, give the class a uniform grid to work with, and be more easily evaluated by you and the students.

AUDIENCE ANALYSIS

To be used first in connection with Assignment 7–2, "Audience Analysis for a Speech to Inform," and for any subsequent assignments or activities requiring an audience analysis. Students have several speech assignments that specifically call for preparing an audience analysis. They should be encouraged to prepare an analysis for all presentations. Although each speech will be different, the procedure for preparing an audience analysis is always quite similar, and a form like this one may be of help to students.

OUTLINE FOR INFORMATIVE SPEECHES

To be used first in connection with Assignment 8–12, "Practice Outline Using Chronology," and for any subsequent informative speech assignments or activities (including demonstration speeches) requiring an outline. Students present several informative speeches. Establishing a uniform outline procedure will help students and may be of classroom management help to you. You may wish to modify this form by adding subpoints (A., B., C., 1., 2., 3., etc.).

CUTTING A SCENE

To be used in connection with Assignments 13–7, "Preparing Yourself and Your Reading," 13–12, "Preparing a Play Cutting," and any other assignments or activities related to oral interpretation. This form can be used by students when cutting various forms of prose, including plays, novels, short stories, or biographies.

CHARACTER ANALYSIS

To be used in connection with Assignment 14–5, "Character Analysis," and with any other assignments or activities related to characterization as a part of storytelling. This form will be of use to students telling stories in which characters are important, especially when there are a number of characters to be differentiated.

LIBRARY OR MEDIA CENTER SURVEY

To be used in connection with Activity 15–D, "Library or Media Center Survey" (at end of Chapter 15, "Defining and Locating Information"). This survey helps students locate major sources of information that will be helpful in securing data for speeches. Because of the amount of outside research required, the Library or Media Center Survey is an optional exercise for Chapter 15; however, it is one the author strongly recommends because of its continued usefulness for the students.

OUTLINE FOR PERSUASIVE SPEECHES

To be used in connection with Assignment 18–7, "Preparing a Speech to Persuade," and for any subsequent persuasive speech assignments or activities requiring an outline. You may wish to modify this form by adding subpoints (A., B., C., 1., 2., 3., etc.).

SELF-INVENTORY

To be used in connection with Assignments 19–1, "Self-Inventory," and 19–9, "Updating Your Self-Inventory." In Chapter 19, "Problem Solving in Groups," students are asked to make two self-evaluations as a result of performances in discussion activities and to compare differences and similarities in their responses to questions.

"Know Thyself": The Personal Inventory

Name _____ Date _____

1. **Vital Data**

   a. Name _____

   b. Nickname _____

   c. Your preferred name _____

   d. Your age and birthdate _____

2. **Family Date**

   a. Members of your family _____

   b. Occupation of father or guardian _____

   c. Occupation of mother or guardian _____

   d. Pets _____

3. **Experiences**

   a. Education: List schools you have attended _____

   _____

   _____

   b. Work: List jobs you have done _____

   _____

   _____

   c. Travel: List places you have visited _____

   _____

   _____

   d. Social: Do you date? Do you belong to any social clubs? Do you belong to any community organizations?

   _____

   _____

e. Recreation: What do you do for "fun"? _____

_____

_____

f. Hobbies: List your hobbies _____

_____

_____

g. Reading: List recent books, newspapers, magazines you have read _____

_____

_____

h. Television: List favorite TV programs _____

_____

_____

i. Music: List types of music you listen to. What are your favorite songs or groups? _____

_____

_____

j. Sports: List ones you play and ones you watch _____

_____

_____

4. **Values:** List the ten most important things, persons, or beliefs in your life _____

_____

_____

5. **Short-Term Goals:** What things do you want to accomplish in the near future? _____

_____

_____

6. **Long-Term Goals:** What do you want to accomplish in your lifetime? _____

_____

_____

7. **Problems:** What are your most immediate and pressing problems? _____

_____

_____

8. **Communication Skills:** What do you see as your communication strengths and weaknesses? _____

_____

_____

9. **Things You Would Like to Change**

   a. What in your world you would like to change _____

   _____

   b. What about yourself you would like to change _____

   _____

10. **Being in School:** What are your feelings about your school and education? _____

_____

_____

11. **Friendship:** What does friendship mean to you? _____

_____

_____

12. **Likes and Dislikes**

   a. Things you like most _____

   _____

   b. Things you dislike most _____

   _____

13. **Self-Portrait:** Write a paragraph describing how you see, feel, and think about yourself _____

_____

_____

_____

Fear Inventory

Name _____ **Date** _____

	My Reactions	**Class Reactions**

A. Physical reactions I experience when faced with situations that really matter:

1. _____ Increased heartbeat _____
2. _____ Cold hands _____
3. _____ Cold feet _____
4. _____ Increased rate of breathing _____
5. _____ Shortness of breath _____
6. _____ Difficulty in breathing _____
7. _____ Tenseness _____
8. _____ Nervousness _____
9. _____ Trembling _____
10. _____ Squeaky voice _____
11. _____ Hoarse voice _____
12. _____ Wrong words come out _____
13. _____ Feel warm all over _____
14. _____ Hot hands _____
15. _____ Hot face _____
16. _____ Blushing _____
17. _____ Dry mouth _____
18. _____ Wet mouth _____
19. _____ Hair stands on end (goosebumps) _____
20. _____ Tingling spine _____
21. _____ Increased perspiration _____
22. _____ Feeling of butterflies in stomach _____
23. _____ Cramps _____
24. _____ Sinking feeling in stomach _____
25. _____ Stomach noises _____

(continued)

Other physical reactions I experience: (list)

_____   _____

_____   _____

_____   _____

_____   _____

_____   _____

B. Feelings and thoughts I experience when faced with situations that really matter:

1. _____ Want to run away   _____

2. _____ Feel like sleeping   _____

3. _____ Daydream about taking trips   _____

4. _____ Think: "Something's wrong with me"   _____

5. _____ Think: "I'm inferior to others"   _____

6. _____ Think: "I'm a coward"   _____

7. _____ Think: "No one else is like this"   _____

8. _____ Think: "Others are better"   _____

9. _____ Think: "Others will think I'm dumb"   _____

10. _____ Think: "Others will think I'm bragging"   _____

11. _____ Think: "I won't have anything to say"   _____

12. _____ Think: "What I want to say is not
              very interesting or important"   _____

13. _____ Think: "I am dumb"   _____

14. _____ Feel silly   _____

15. _____ Feel clumsy   _____

16. _____ Feel I shouldn't be like this   _____

Other thoughts and feelings I have: (list)

_____

_____

_____

_____

C. Situations that I think really matter:

1. _____ A game or race (sports)   _____

2. _____ A performance (music or theatre)   _____

3. _____ Giving a speech   _____

4. _____ Calling for a date   _____

5. _____ Waiting for a date to arrive   _____

6. _____ A big social event (dance, party, etc.)   _____

7. _____ Play tryouts   _____

8. _____ Examination, test, or quiz   _____

9. _____ Writing themes or papers   _____

10. _____ An election in which I'm a candidate   _____

11. _____ Interviews   _____

12. _____ Going to a dentist   _____

13. _____ Going to a doctor   _____

14. _____ Leaving on vacation   _____

15. _____ Meeting important people for the first time _____

Other situations that produce fear reactions in me: (list)

_____

_____

_____

_____

_____

Characteristics of Success

Name _____ **Date** _____

List five times in your life that you felt successful. Then check the characteristics of success that apply to each of your personal successes. Next, total the number of times you checked each characteristic, and write the total in the right-hand column. Circle the characteristics that you marked most frequently—these are your "satisfiers."

1. _____

2. _____

3. _____

4. _____

5. _____

SUCCESSES						TOTALS (number of times this item checked)
1	2	3	4	5		
					Independence (working on my own)	
					Hard work	
					Curiosity	
					Artistic ability	
					Growing, preparing, cooking food	
					Concentration	
					Memory	
					Leadership	
					Organizing	
					Follow-through	
					Building or making something	
					Design (using space, form, color)	
					Human relations	

(continued)

SUCCESSES						TOTALS (number of times this item checked)
1	2	3	4	5		
					Speaking	
					Record keeping	
					Planning	
					Persuasion	
					Serving or helping people	
					Health, personal appearance	
					Adapting to change	
					Initiative	
					Ideas and thinking	
					Love, acceptance from others	
					Outdoor activity	
					Routine	
					Research and analysis	
					Travel	
					Observation	
					Self-respect	
					Ownership	
					Exploring new ideas	
					Performing (singing, acting, playing)	
					Income	
					Managing money	
					Creativity	
					Using numbers, statistics, figures	
					Working with others cooperatively	

SUCCESSES

	1	2	3	4	5		
						Attention to detail	
						Fixing or repairing	
						Problem solving	
						Managing conflict	
						Planning ahead	
						Recognition by others	
						Physical energy	
						Excitement, daring, taking chances	

Audience Analysis Form

Name _____ **Date of Speech** _____

Title of Speech _____

_____

General Purpose of Speech _____

_____

Specific Purpose of Speech _____

Central Theme _____

Occasion _____

Number of listeners _____ Number of males _____ Number of females _____

Age(s) of listeners _____

Needs of audience _____

_____

Audience's degree of interest in subject _____

_____

Audience's knowledge of subject _____

_____

Audience's attitude toward subject _____

_____

Audience's attitude toward me _____

_____

How is introduction suited to this audience? _____

_____

What kind of audience contact language would be appropriate? _____

_____

What examples can I use that would relate to this audience? _____

_____

_____

What else can I do to make sure this audience will feel that I am speaking directly to them, for their benefit?

_____

_____

_____

Outline for Informative Speech

Name _____ **Date of Speech** _____

Title of Speech _____

I. Introduction (time _____) Give audience a clear statement of subject. Tell them why they need the information. Let them know why you are qualified speaker on this topic. Use one of the four types of organization discussed in Chapter 7.

_____

_____

_____

_____

_____

_____

_____

_____

_____

II. Body of Speech (time _____)

_____

_____

_____

_____

_____

_____

_____

_____

_____

_____

_____

_____

_____

_____

_____

_____

_____

_____

_____

III. Conclusion (time _____) Summarize the main ideas. Restate the value the audience should get from the information. Prepare a snappy, forceful punch line, using one of the methods mentioned in Chapter 7.

_____

_____

_____

_____

_____

_____

_____

_____

_____

_____

Cutting a Scene

Name _____ **Date** _____

Title _____ **Author** _____

In selecting a scene ask these questions:

1. Does the scene present an adequate example of:

    a. The story? _____

    b. The characters? _____

    c. The mood? _____

    d. The locale? _____

2. Does the scene have action? _____

3. Does the scene have a climax? _____

4. Does the climax involve action or is it psychological? _____

5. Why did you select this scene? _____

    _____

6. What is the relationship between this scene and the rest of the selection? _____

    _____

7. What is the theme of this selection? _____

    _____

8. How does the scene you have chosen represent that theme? _____

    _____

9. Describe the characters in the scene you have selected. _____

    _____

10. Describe the setting of the scene you have selected. _____

    _____

11. What types of voices are required of the characters? _____

    _____

12. What is the main idea, thought, or feeling you want this selection to communicate? _____

_____

Prepare an outline for your reading that includes the following information: title and author of selection; important facts about the author; central theme of the selection; time and place of the action; type of action; characters; summary of the story up to the point where the reading begins.

_____

_____

_____

_____

_____

Character Analysis

Name _____ **Date** _____

Build your own mental picture of the characters in your story. In the spaces below write the key words that describe the pictures you have of these characters.

Character (name, age, sex)	Voice	Physical Appearance (posture, gestures, dress)	Typical Language Character Uses (phrases, slang, language that reveals educational level)

Library or Media Center Survey

Name _____ **Date** _____

A. General Information

1. Name and location of library or media center

   _____

   _____

2. Hours of service

   _____

3. Name of head librarian and general information phone number

   _____

4. Name of reference librarian(s) and reference phone number

   _____

5. Does the library have a set of rules? _____ (If so, obtain a copy and include it in your Activity Notebook.)

B. Printed Material

6. Where is the card catalog located?

   _____ In cabinets

   _____ On microfilm or microfiche

   _____ On computer

   Do you know how to use the card catalog? _____ (If not, ask the librarian for assistance and take notes.)

7. Where is the reference department located?

   _____

8. Survey the reference department. Can you locate the following materials?

   _____ *Readers' Guide to Periodical Literature*

   _____ *Index to Periodical Literature*

   _____ *Education Index*

   _____ *New York Times Index*

   What other kinds of indexes are available?

   _____

9. Do you know how to use the *Readers' Guide to Periodical Literature?* _____ (If not, ask the reference librarian for assistance and take notes.) Write down the location of three different articles that you found using the *Readers' Guide.*

   _____

   _____

10. Which of the following research tools can be found in the library?

_____ *Encyclopaedia Britannica*

_____ *Encyclopedia Americana*

_____ *World Book Encyclopedia*

_____ *Encyclopedia of the Social Sciences*

List two other research tools that you located.

_____

_____

11. Which of the following sources of statistics can be found in the library?

_____ *World Almanac*

_____ *Information Please Almanac*

_____ *Statistical Abstracts of the United States*

What other statistical sources can you find?

_____

_____

12. Does the library have an open-shelf or closed-stacks policy?

_____

13. For how long a period can you check out the following?

Books _____

Reserved books _____

Periodicals _____

Reserved periodicals _____

Encyclopedias _____

How often can you renew any of these items, and for how long?

_____

_____

C. Other Media

Many library and resource centers contain a variety of useful materials for providing you with information and for helping you present information.

14. Determine which of the following are available

_____ videocassette recorders (VCRs)	_____ filmstrip collection
_____ video cameras (camcorders)	_____ movie projectors
_____ videocassette collection	_____ film (movie) library
_____ audiocassette recorders (tape recorders)	_____ overhead projectors
_____ record/CD players	_____ opaque projectors

_____ music library (recordings)   _____ personal computers

_____ filmstrip projectors   _____ computer software

15. What other materials are available from the library or media center that might be useful in presenting information to others?

_____

_____

_____

_____

16. Is there a computerized data base? If so, which one(s)? How do you use it?

_____

_____

_____

_____

D. Other Resource Centers

17. What other libraries exist in your community that might be open to you (for example, theatre library, business library, museum library)?

_____

_____

_____

18. Does your state government support a library? If so, where is it located and what are the procedures for using it?

_____

_____

_____

19. What is the Library of Congress? What kinds of information are available there that might not be available in your local libraries?

_____

_____

_____

20. The U.S. government publishes hundreds of pamphlets, books, and articles. Many of these are free. Locate the address for requesting information about U.S. government publications. (You may wish to request a catalog.)

_____

_____

_____

Outline for Persuasive Speech

Name _____ **Date of Speech** _____

Title of Speech _____

Audience _____

   I. Introduction (time _____) Use as attention-getting device and plan to deliver your introduction verbatim.

      _____

      _____

      _____

      _____

  II. The Nature of the Problem (time _____) Use outline form.

    A. The Effects _____

      _____

      _____

      _____

    B. The Extent _____

      _____

      _____

      _____

    C. The Causes _____

      _____

      _____

      _____

 III. The Solution (time _____)

      _____

      _____

      _____

      _____

IV. The Visualization of the Solution (time _____)

_____

_____

_____

_____

_____

_____

V. Conclusion (time _____) Appeal to the audience for action. Plan to deliver your conclusion
verbatim.

_____

_____

_____

_____

_____

_____

Self-Inventory

Name _____ **Date** _____

Read the following questions and write an X next to the ones that apply to your feelings and behavior.

_____ 1. Am I fearful of being wrong?

_____ 2. Do I speak clearly?

_____ 3. Do I ask questions when I have them?

_____ 4. Do I ask questions just to get attention?

_____ 5. Do I speak forcefully enough to be heard?

_____ 6. Do I stick to my point?

_____ 7. Do I stick to my point just to defend my ego?

_____ 8. Am I usually prepared?

_____ 9. Do I look directly at people when I speak to them?

_____ 10. Do I listen carefully?

_____ 11. Does my mind wander when others speak?

_____ 12. Are my thoughts well organized when I present them?

_____ 13. Am I willing to compromise?

_____ 14. Am I too willing to compromise?

_____ 15. Do I talk too much?

_____ 16. Do I tend to dominate a group?

_____ 17. Do I give in too easily on an issue?

_____ 18. Do I have strong and unsupported prejudices?

_____ 19. Do I arrive on time?

_____ 20. Am I sincere?

_____ 21. Do I feel I am a worthwhile person?

_____ 22. Do I make my ideas clear by using examples or illustrations?

_____ 23. Am I objective in my problem-solving attitude?

_____ 24. Am I able to approach others and make them feel welcome and worthwhile?

_____ 25. Do I know the steps of critical thinking?

Part Four
Supplemental Assessment Tools

SPEAKING BY DOING: CHAPTER CHECKUP QUESTIONS

The following blackline masters (Chapter Checkups) may be used to assist in assessing students' comprehension of the text and their growth as communicators. A Chapter Checkup is provided for each of the twenty chapters in the student edition.

Chapter Checkup

Chapter 1 Introduction

Name _____ **Date** _____

For each question below, write a paragraph or two to explain your answer with specific facts, examples, and/or illustrations.

1. How does human communication depend on the use of symbols?

2. Why is it important for people to set their own goals?

3. Explain the role of spoken language in each of your "lives":

   a. personal

   b. work

   c. social

Chapter Checkup
Chapter 2 Nature and Purposes of Speech Communication

Name _____ **Date** _____

For each question below, write a paragraph or two to explain your answer with specific facts, examples, and/or illustrations.

1. What are some forms and purposes of self-talk? How is self-talk useful or helpful to us?

2. Create a scenario—a situation with people in it—that illustrates the steps of the communication process. Label each step in the illustration.

3. What is feedback? How is it important to speakers and listeners? What questions does it answer?

Chapter Checkup

Chapter 3 Getting Acquainted in a New Community

Name _____ **Date** _____

Create a specific speaking situation that includes a speaker, audience, topic, purpose, and occasion. For this situation, what three areas of the Audience Analysis Form are likely to be most important? Explain your answers by relating each area to the speaking situation.

Situation:

    speaker:

    audience:

    topic:

    purpose:

    occasion:

Area A.

Area B.

Area C.

Chapter Checkup

Chapter 4 Social Conversation

Name _____ **Date** _____

For each question below, write a paragraph or two to explain your answer with specific facts, examples, and/or illustrations.

1. How is conversation different from two people taking turns talking to each other? How would the outcomes of these two circumstances be likely to differ? Use an illustration to develop your answers.

2. Create two situations for which introductions are needed. For one, write a poor introduction that does not begin a conversation. For the other, write a good introduction, one that opens up a conversation between the people introduced.

   Situation A:

   Poor Introduction:

   Situation B:

   Good Introduction:

Chapter Checkup

Chapter 5 Speech Fears and Self-Confidence

Name _____ **Date** _____

Below are seven common misconceptions about fear. For each, explain why the idea is a misconception, and then give an example or illustration to show a more accurate view.

1. Self-confidence means the same as not being afraid.

2. Fear is bad and should be eliminated.

3. When a person is afraid, it is a sign of weakness or inferiority.

4. Persons who do things well do them without being afraid.

5. Brave persons do not have fear; only cowards are afraid.

6. Self-confidence comes suddenly one day, and fear no longer exists.

7. Pain is a bad and undesirable experience.

Chapter Checkup

Chapter 6 Speech Communication and Your Future

Name _____ **Date** _____

A friend who is about to interview for a job has asked you for help in preparing for the experience. Your friend's question is this: "What kinds of questions might the interviewer ask me?" Below are seven types of questions your friend might encounter. For **five** of these question types, explain the form of question and give your friend an example of the type.

Starter question

Open-ended question

Follow-up question

Direct information question

Yes/no question

Forced-choice question

Telling-back question

Chapter Checkup

Chapter 7 Contexts, Audiences, Topics, and Purposes

Name _____ Date _____

For each question below, write a paragraph or two to explain your answer with specific facts, examples, and/or illustrations.

1. What is meant by the term "rhetorical situation"? What is the importance of the rhetorical situation in any speech or presentation?

2. Give examples of one-way and two-way communication contexts.

3. Starting with the general topic "sports," write three specific topics—one for information, one for demonstration, and one for persuasion. Then, write three very general outlines by using the frameworks below.

Information topic:

Topic

Aspect 1

Aspect 2

Aspect 3

Application

Demonstration topic:

Rationale

Step 1

Step 2

Step 3

Step 4

Application

Persuasion topic:

Problem

Effects

Causes

Solution

Benefits

Chapter Checkup
Chapter 8 Writing for Success: Using the Tricks of the Trade

Name _____ **Date** _____

For each technique listed below, explain where and how you might use it in a speech or presentation.

1. giving examples

2. telling jokes or stories

3. using a quotation

4. making an analogy

5. giving a series of facts

6. making a shocking statement

7. using a visual or sound or prop

8. organizing by time or chronology

9. organizing by space

10. organizing by structure

11. organizing by function

12. organizing by cause and effect

13. organizing by quantity, size, or scope

14. organizing by quality, importance, or cost

Chapter Checkup

Chapter 9 Your Voice and Its Powers

Name _____ **Date** _____

Effective use of your voice depends on five factors. Explain the importance of each factor listed below, and then write a summary statement that explains how these factors work together to produce an effective presentation.

Controlled breathing:

Clear articulation:

Increased volume and projection:

Proper inflection and emphasis:

Good pronunciation:

Summary statement:

Chapter Checkup
Chapter 10 Using Body Language

Name _____ **Date** _____

Illustrate the importance of nonverbal behavior by comparing and contrasting two speakers—one who is non-verbally effective and another who is not—in the same situation. Be sure to comment on all aspects listed below for both speakers, and explain why what each does is effective or ineffective. Begin by creating a specific situation.

1. Speaking Situation

   Speaker:

   Audience:

   Topic:

   Purpose:

   Occasion:

2. Ineffective Speaker

   Physical Appearance:

   Posture:

   Eye Contact:

   Gestures:

3. Effective Speaker

   Physical Appearance:

   Posture:

   Eye Contact:

   Gestures:

Chapter Checkup
Chapter 11 Using Support Materials

Name _____ **Date** _____

For each question below, write a paragraph or two to explain your answer with specific facts, examples, and/or illustrations.

1. Identify two kinds of handouts and explain their typical uses or applications in a speech or presentation.

    A.

    B.

2. Identify two kinds of visual aids and explain their typical uses or applications in a speech or presentation.

    A.

    B.

3. Identify two kinds of audio aids and explain their typical uses or applications in a speech or presentation.

    A.

    B.

Chapter Checkup

Chapter 12 Rehearsing and Monitoring for Success

Name _____ **Date** _____

Tell the story of the series of rehearsals that an experienced speaker might complete to prepare for a successful presentation. Use the Rehearsal Checklist as a guide. Write at least one paragraph for each step on the checklist.

_____ rehearsed in the speaking situation or setting

_____ rehearsed with actual speaking notes

_____ rehearsed with microphone

_____ rehearsed with props, handouts, visuals, etc.

_____ rehearsed Plan B

_____ dress-rehearsed in presentation outfit

_____ rehearsed with response from listener (or audiotape or videotape)

Chapter Checkup
Chapter 13 Oral Interpretation

Name _____ **Date** _____

Select a well-known fairy tale, folktale, legend, fable, story, or song to present orally. Explain how you would handle in your presentation each of the elements of oral interpretation listed below.

Title of Work _____

Plot:

Characters:

Setting:

Conflict:

Chapter Checkup

Chapter 14 Telling a Good Story

Name _____ **Date** _____

How do you decide if a story has been told well? Develop your own Feedback Form for responding to the telling of a story. The form should have at least five questions or headings. List them in the spaces below and write explanations of the importance of each feature and the standard(s) you would use to measure it.

1. _____

2. _____

3. _____

4. _____

5. _____

Chapter Checkup
Chapter 15 Defining and Locating Information

Name _____ **Date** _____

For each question below, write a paragraph or two to explain your answer with specific facts, examples, and/or illustrations.

1. How does information differ from knowledge?

2. What are three important characteristics of information? Explain each.

   A.

   B.

   C.

3. Identify three sources of public knowledge and explain how each is experienced.

   A.

   B.

   C.

Chapter Checkup

Chapter 16 Presenting the Speech to Inform

Name _____ **Date** _____

This chapter presents six guidelines for effective presentation, and then four problems for critical listening. In the spaces below, write two scenarios or story outlines, one for a speaker and the other for a listener. In each case, show how the communicator attends to the guidelines or problems presented in the chapter.

The Speaker (six guidelines):

The Listener (four problems):

Chapter Checkup

Chapter 17 The Demonstration Speech

Name _____ **Date** _____

A friend, an inexperienced speaker, has come to you for advice. He or she must demonstrate a familiar process to classmates. In the space that follows, write a conversation (a dialogue) with your friend. In the conversation, explain all six steps of this preparation sequence:

- prepare audience analysis
- select topic
- gather and organize materials, prepare speech
- practice speech
- present speech
- receive and evaluate feedback

Be sure to specify not only what to do but also how to do it.

Chapter Checkup

Chapter 18 Speaking to Persuade

Name _____ **Date** _____

Below are six types of groups. Using an imaginary individual, show how he or she belongs to at least five of these groups. You may identify smaller groups within these larger categories. Suggest some responsibilities of membership in each group.

1. Social Groups

2. Economic Groups

3. Political Groups

4. Religious Groups

5. Educational Groups

6. Military and Law Enforcement Groups

Chapter Checkup

Chapter 19 Problem Solving in Groups

Name _____ **Date** _____

Use the nine-step process outlined below to work out a solution to a real or imaginary personal problem. Give specific details for each step.

1. Need is felt

2. Need is located

3. Need is defined

4. Need is analyzed

5. All possible solutions are considered

6. One solution is selected

7. The solution is put into operation

8. The solution is given continued evaluation

9. Changes, adaptations, or new solutions are put into operation

Chapter Checkup

Chapter 20 Parliamentary Procedure

Name _____ **Date** _____

For each question below, write a paragraph or two to explain your answer with specific facts, examples, and/or illustrations.

1. Why do groups use parliamentary procedure? What are some benefits?

2. Explain the purpose or duties of each of the following elements:

   A. a constitution

   B. the chairperson

   C. the secretary

   D. the minutes

   E. a main motion

   F. a secondary motion

A NOTE ABOUT ASSESSMENT

The suggestions that follow are not model answers to the questions. Instead, they are short lists of content criteria for effective responses. We do not include criteria for organization, sentence structure, grammar, punctuation, and mechanics.

Further, certain criteria are common to most questions. "Elaboration" or "degree of detail," for example, is a quality of a good answer to most essay questions, and so it is here. You might share with students—at the beginning of the course—these general criteria for all written responses, and then use the more specific criteria that follow to respond to and/or evaluate work on the Chapter Checkup Questions. Some general criteria:

- focus on accomplishing the task
- elaboration or degree of detail
- organization or order of presentation
- clarity of expression
- control of conventions and mechanics

Our approach here is to suggest what effective answers to each question would be likely to include. The questions are designed to produce an array of responses, so it is likely that instructors will see very different—yet equally effective—responses to the same question. We assume every instructor will be looking for focused, clear, organized responses. Our suggestions, then, are directed toward specific content requirements and characteristics.

CHAPTER CHECKUP/SUGGESTED RESPONSES

CHAPTER 1 INTRODUCTION

1. Explain the role of spoken language in each of your "lives":
   a. personal
   b. work
   c. social

Effective responses will:
- show that communication is important in most life situations
- show that leadership and success are related to language ability
- give a specific, personal example of spoken language impact on personal, work, and social "lives."

2. What are some advantages of setting your own goals?

Effective responses will:
- note that people learn best when they have an interest in their growth and development
- show that knowledge of the "game" can help a player to improve specific skills
- suggest that goal setting is an incentive to achievement and an early step in assessment or evaluation

CHAPTER 2 NATURE AND PURPOSES OF SPEECH COMMUNICATION

1. What are some forms and purposes of self-talk? How is self-talk useful or helpful to us?

Effective responses will:
- include such forms as thinking, planning, organizing, daydreaming, imagining, listening, and making decisions
- list such uses as problem solving, exploring, brainstorming, motivating, and learning

2. Create a scenario—a situation with people in it—that illustrates the steps of the communication process. Label each step in the illustration.

Effective responses will:
- give a specfic situation that includes and labels each of these steps:
    1. speaker begins process (need or want)
    2. speaker creates or encodes message
    3. speaker selects channel
    4. speaker sends or transmits message
    5. listener receives message
    6. listener interprets or decodes message
    7. listener plans and sends feedback
    8. original speaker, now listener, interprets feedback
    9. original speaker adjusts first message

3. What is feedback? How is it important to speakers and listeners? What questions does it answer?

Effective responses will:
- note that only with feedback can a speaker adapt to varying conditions of listeners
- show that feedback allows a speaker to know if he or she is being received, understood, and/or accepted (three questions)

CHAPTER 3 GETTING ACQUAINTED IN A NEW COMMUNITY

Create a specific speaking situation that includes a speaker, audience, topic, purpose, and occasion. For this situation, what three areas of the Audience Analysis

Form are likely to be most important? Explain your answers by relating each area to the speaking situation.

Situation:

speaker:

audience:

topic:

purpose:

occasion:

Effective responses will:
- give specific detail about all five aspects of the speaking situation
- directly relate three of these areas to the speaking situation:

size of audience

gender distribution

age distribution

common needs

common interests

common experiences
- give a reason each of the three would be important in this situation

CHAPTER 4 SOCIAL CONVERSATION

1. How is conversation different from two people taking turns talking to each other? How would the outcomes of these two circumstances be likely to differ? Use an illustration to develop your answers.

Effective responses will:
- show that the key difference is that listening is essential to the dialogue of conversation, while the other situation is more like two monologues
- suggest that conversation, because it involves listening, can lead to learning, change, and new understanding
- develop these ideas with an illustration (or several)

2. Create two situations for which introductions are needed. For one, write a poor introduction that does not begin a conversation. For the other, write a good introduction, one that opens up a conversation between the people introduced.

Effective responses will:
- develop ideas through two situations with adequate information
- include a poor introduction that is flat, impersonal, and directionless
- include a good introduction that contains a conversation opener to link the people being introduced

CHAPTER 5 SPEECH FEARS AND SELF-CONFIDENCE

Below are seven common misconceptions about fear. For each, explain why the idea is a misconception, and then give an example or illustration to show a more accurate view

1. Self-confidence means the same as not being afraid.
2. Fear is bad and should be eliminated.
3. When a person is afraid, it is a sign of weakness or inferiority.
4. Persons who do things well do them without being afraid.
5. Brave persons do not have fear; only cowards are afraid.
6. Self-confidence comes suddenly one day, and fear no longer exists.
7. Pain is a bad and undesirable experience.

Effective responses will:
- point out why each statement is incorrect, misleading, or incomplete
- develop an example to show a more complete or accurate view of the concept

Note: These misconceptions are treated in detail in Chapter 5.

CHAPTER 6 SPEECH COMMUNICATION AND YOUR FUTURE

A friend who is about to interview for a job has asked you for help in preparing for the experience. Your friend's question is this: "What kinds of questions might the interviewer ask me?" Below are seven types of questions your friend might encounter. For **five** of these question types, explain the form of question and give your friend an example of the type.

Starter question
Open-ended question
Follow-up question
Direct information question
Yes/no question
Forced-choice question
Telling-back question

Effective responses will:
- give a clear explanation of what each question (of five) is like and what kind of information it tries to elicit
- provide an example of each question type

Note: Chapter 6 contains explanations and many examples of each question type.

CHAPTER 7 CONTEXTS, AUDIENCES, TOPICS, AND PURPOSES

1. What is meant by the term "rhetorical situation"? What is the importance of the rhetorical situation in any speech or presentation?

Effective responses will:
- explain the term as the speaking context—who is talking to whom, about what, and for what purposes
- show that this context must be understood before a speaker can plan content, organization, style, etc.

2. Give examples of one-way and two-way communication contexts.

Effective responses will:
- identify television, radio, newspaper, etc. as one-way contexts
- identify telephone and live conversations, debates, panel discussions, etc. as two-way contexts

3. Starting with the general topic "sports," write three specific topics—one for information, one for demonstration, and one for persuasion. Then, write three very general outlines by using the frameworks below.

Information topic:
Topic
Aspect 1
Aspect 2
Aspect 3
Application

Demonstration topic:
Rationale
Step 1
Step 2
Step 3
Step 4
Application

Persuasion topic:
Problem
Effects
Causes
Solution
Benefits

Effective responses will:
- shape the general topic of "sports" into three different specific topics such as:

Information Topic	"My Favorite Sports"
Demonstration Topic	"How to Start Your Own Fitness Program"
Persuasion Topic	"Overpaying Players is Ruining Professional Sports"

- follow the three organizing frameworks by writing one point (or sentence) for each part
- provide a focus for each outline:

Information	tell about something
Demonstration	show how to do something
Persuasion	call for action

CHAPTER 8 WRITING FOR SUCCESS: USING THE TRICKS OF THE TRADE

For each technique listed below, explain where and how you might use it in a speech or presentation.

1. giving examples
2. telling jokes or stories
3. using a quotation
4. making an analogy
5. giving a series of facts
6. making a shocking statement
7. using a visual or sound or prop
8. organizing by time or chronology
9. organizing by space
10. organizing by structure
11. organizing by function
12. organizing by cause and effect
13. organizing by quantity, size, or scope
14. organizing by quality, importance, or cost

Effective responses will:
- describe the purpose or structure of the technique and the specific place in the speech where it would be used
- give a reason for its effectiveness in that place

Note: Each technique is treated in detail in Chapter 8.

CHAPTER 9 YOUR VOICE AND ITS POWERS

Effective use of your voice depends on five factors. Explain the importance of each factor listed blow, and then write a summary statement that explains how these factors work together to produce an effective presentation.

Controlled breathing:
Clear articulation:
Increased volume and projection:
Proper inflection and emphasis:
Good pronunciation:
Summary statement:

Effective responses will:
- explain the importance of each factor, give examples, and demonstrate an understanding of the terms (how inflection differs from emphasis)
- in the summary statement, synthesize the factors to show they work together to produce a strong, clear, pleasing voice

CHAPTER 10 USING BODY LANGUAGE

Illustrate the importance of nonverbal behavior by comparing and contrasting two speakers—one who is nonverbally effective and another who is not—in the same situation. Be sure to comment on all aspects listed below for both speakers, and explain why what each does is effective or ineffective. Begin by creating a specific situation.

1. Speaking Situation

   Speaker:
   Audience:
   Topic:
   Purpose:
   Occasion:

2. Ineffective Speaker

   Physical Appearance:
   Posture:
   Eye Contact:
   Gestures:

3. Effective Speaker

   Physical Appearance:
   Posture:
   Eye Contact:
   Gestures:

Effective responses will:
- identify all five aspects of the speaking situation
- for each of the four nonverbal features, provide a clear contrast between the practices and results of the ineffective speaker and those of the effective speaker
- use specific language in each explanation to demonstrate clear understanding of the practices involved ("poor eye contact" is not specific language; "reads from a manuscript and never looks up at the audience" is specific language)
- illustrate that nonverbal communication is built into a presentation, not just added on

CHAPTER 11 USING SUPPORT MATERIALS

1. Identify two kinds of handouts and explain their typical uses or applications in a speech or presentation.

Effective responses will:
- identify and explain uses for two of these types of handouts: outline, open outline, significant figures, multi-page, response, and question
- use specific language in examples or illustrations

2. Identify two kinds of visual aids and explain their typical uses or applications in a speech or presentation.

Effective responses will:
- identify and explain the uses of two of these types of visual aids: photos, movies, models, art forms, props and people, graphs, charts, drawings, and computer graphics
- use specific language in examples or illustrations

3. Identify two kinds of audio aids and explain their typical uses or applications in a speech or presentation.

Effective responses will:
- identify and explain the uses of two of these types of audio aids: recordings (of various types) and objects themselves
- use specific language in examples or illustrations

CHAPTER 12 REHEARSING AND MONITORING FOR SUCCESS

Tell the story of the series of rehearsals that an experienced speaker might complete to prepare for a successful presentation. Use the Rehearsal Checklist as a guide. Write at least one paragraph for each step on the checklist.

_____ rehearsed in the speaking situation or setting
_____ rehearsed with actual speaking notes
_____ rehearsed with microphone
_____ rehearsed with props, handouts, visuals, etc.
_____ rehearsed Plan B
_____ dress-rehearsed in presentation outfit
_____ rehearsed with response from listener (or audiotape or videotape)

Effective responses will:
- create a detailed "story" that illustrates each level of rehearsal or preparation for a presentation
- provide specific information to demonstrate understanding of the connections among these rehearsal types

CHAPTER 13 ORAL INTERPRETATION

Select a well-known fairy tale, folktale, legend, fable, story, or song to present orally. Explain how you would handle in your presentation each of the elements of oral interpretation listed below.

Title of Work _____
Plot:
Characters:
Setting:
Conflict:

Effective responses will:
- separate the four elements and analyze each in turn
- provide specific information on speaker's techniques and decisions
- show an understanding of the connections among these literary elements
- use appropriate terms ("climax")

CHAPTER 14 TELLING A GOOD STORY

How do you decide if a story has been told well? Develop your own Feedback Form for responding to the telling of a story. The form should have at least five questions or headings. List them in the spaces below and write explanations of the importance of each feature and the standard(s) you would use to measure it.

Effective responses will:
- identify at least five criteria for good storytelling and explain the importance of each—these might include technical and content criteria
- for each criterion, suggest a range from high to low or good to poor

CHAPTER 15 DEFINING AND LOCATING INFORMATION

1. How does information differ from knowledge?

Effective responses will:
- show that knowledge is produced when information has been connected, related, or assimilated in such a way that it can be used
- give an example to distinguish between the two concepts

2. What are three important characteristics of information? Explain each.

Effective responses will:
- present the three concepts of accuracy, newness, and usefulness to listeners
- explain each concept with an example or illustration

3. Identify three sources of public knowledge and explain how each is experienced.

Effective responses will:
- identify three of the following sources: museums, galleries, libraries and media centers, information retrieval systems, computer networks
- give an example or explanation of how each is used or experienced

CHAPTER 16 PRESENTING THE SPEECH TO INFORM

This chapter presents seven guidelines for effective presentation, and then four problems for critical listening. In the spaces below, write two scenarios or story outlines, one for a speaker and the other for a listener. In each case, show how the communicator attends to the guidelines or problems presented in the chapter.

Effective responses will:
- present an example or narrative that involves these guidelines for the speaker: get audience's attention, be visible, use good posture, speak up, use repetition, be conversational, use a strong ending
- show how the speaker does these in practice
- present a second example or narrative that deals with these problems for critical listening: observing repetition, distinguishing fact from opinion, making connections, wrapping it up (getting the summary)
- show how the listener does these in practice

CHAPTER 17 THE DEMONSTRATION SPEECH

A friend, an inexperienced speaker, has come to you for advice. He or she must demonstrate a familiar process to classmates. In the space that follows, write a conversation (a dialogue) with your friend. In the conversation, explain all six steps of this preparation sequence:

- prepare audience analysis
- select topic
- gather and organize materials, prepare speech
- practice speech
- present speech
- receive and evaluate feedback

Be sure to specify not only what to do but also how to do it.

Effective responses will:
- take the form of a dialogue or conversation between the inexperienced speaker and the more experienced speaker
- develop all six steps through the conversation
- explain what each step means and tell what to do for that step
- also tell how to go about it

CHAPTER 18 SPEAKING TO PERSUADE

Below are six types of groups. Using an imaginary individual, show how he or she belongs to at least five of these groups. You may identify smaller groups within these larger categories. Suggest some responsibilities of membership in each group.

1. Social Groups
2. Economic Groups
3. Political Groups
4. Religious Groups
5. Educational Groups
6. Military and Law Enforcement Groups

Effective responses will:
- involve membership in five groups in the discussion and classify each type of group mentioned (family = Social Group)
- show the imaginary individual's participation in each
- suggest the overlapping—perhaps even conflicting—nature of membership in so many types of groups

CHAPTER 19 PROBLEM SOLVING IN GROUPS

Use the nine-step process outlined below to work out a solution to a real or imaginary personal problem. Give specific details for each step.

1. need is felt
2. need is located
3. need is defined
4. need is analyzed
5. all possible solutions are considered
6. one solution is selected
7. the solution is put into operation

8. the solution is given continued evaluation
9. changes, adaptations, or new solutions are put into operation

Effective responses will:
- work through a real or imaginary personal problem by using all nine steps
- give specific details as facts, examples, or illustrations for each step
- demonstrate an understanding of the flow of the problem-solving process

CHAPTER 20 PARLIAMENTARY PROCEDURE

1. Why do groups use parliamentary procedure? What are some benefits?

Effective responses will:
- show that large groups that make important decisions may need to use "governed decision making"
- show that group members' differences in values, power, and needs make such a system necessary
- suggest such benefits as thoughtful consideration of problems, peaceful resolution by voting, and opportunities to discuss issue and alternatives

2. Explain the purpose for or duties of each of the following elements:

Effective responses will:
- show that a constitution establishes basic agreements for operating the group
- note that the chairperson's chief duty is to conduct meetings: call them to order, direct them in progress, and adjourn them
- tell that the secretary is responsible for the detail work: keep attendance, documents, and records of meetings and decisions
- show that the minutes are the main record of meetings and decisions of the group
- tell that a main motion is a proposal to do something, a call for action, which must be approved by a vote of the membership
- show that secondary motions are procedural: amendments, postponements, limits on debate, calls for vote

Note: Fuller treatment of these elements is given in Chapter 20 of the student text.

NTC LANGUAGE ARTS BOOKS

Business Communication
Handbook for Business Writing, *Baugh, Fryar, & Thomas*
Meetings: Rules & Procedures, *Pohl*

Dictionaries
British/American Language Dictionary, *Moss*
NTC's Classical Dictionary, *Room*
NTC's Dictionary of Changes in Meaning, *Room*
NTC's Dictionary of Debate, *Hanson*
NTC's Dictionary of Literary Terms, *Morner & Rausch*
NTC's Dictionary of Theatre and Drama Terms, *Mobley*
NTC's Dictionary of Word Origins, *Room*
NTC's Spell It Right Dictionary, *Downing*
Robin Hyman's Dictionary of Quotations

Essential Skills
Building Real Life English Skills, *Starkey & Penn*
Developing Creative & Critical Thinking, *Boostrom*
English Survival Series, *Maggs*
Essential Life Skills, *Starkey & Penn*
Essentials of English Grammar, *Baugh*
Essentials of Reading and Writing English Series
Grammar for Use, *Hall*
Grammar Step-by-Step, *Pratt*
Guide to Better English Spelling, *Furness*
How to Be a Rapid Reader, *Redway*
How to Improve Your Study Skills, *Coman & Heavers*
How to Write Term Papers and Reports, *Baugh*
NTC Skill Builders
Reading by Doing, *Simmons & Palmer*
303 Dumb Spelling Mistakes, *Downing*
TIME: We the People, *ed. Schinke-Llano*
Vocabulary by Doing, *Beckert*

Genre Literature
Coming of Age, *Emra*
The Detective Story, *Schwartz*
The Short Story & You, *Simmons & Stern*
Sports in Literature, *Emra*
You and Science Fiction, *Hollister*

Journalism
Getting Started in Journalism, *Harkrider*
Journalism Today! *Ferguson & Patten*
Publishing the Literary Magazine, *Klaiman*
UPI Stylebook, *United Press International*

Language, Literature, and Composition
African American Literature, *Worley & Perry*
An Anthology for Young Writers, *Meredith*
The Art of Composition, *Meredith*
Creative Writing, *Mueller & Reynolds*
Handbook for Practical Letter Writing, *Baugh*
How to Write Term Papers and Reports, *Baugh*

In a New Land, *Grossman & Schur*
Literature by Doing, *Tchudi & Yesner*
Lively Writing, *Schrank*
Look, Think & Write, *Leavitt & Sohn*
NTC Shakespeare Series
NTC Vocabulary Builders
Poetry by Doing, *Osborn*
World Literature, *Rosenberg*
Write to the Point! *Morgan*
The Writer's Handbook, *Karls & Szymanski*
Writing by Doing, *Sohn & Enger*
Writing in Action, *Meredith*

Media Communication
Getting Started in Mass Media, *Beckert*
Photography in Focus, *Jacobs & Kokrda*
Television Production Today!, *Bielak*
Understanding Mass Media, *Schrank*
Understanding the Film, *Bone & Johnson*

Mythology
The Ancient World, *Sawyer & Townsend*
Mythology and You, *Rosenberg & Baker*
Welcome to Ancient Greece, *Millard*
Welcome to Ancient Rome, *Millard*
World Mythology, *Rosenberg*

Speech
Activities for Effective Communication, *LiSacchi*
The Basics of Speech, *Galvin, Cooper, & Gordon*
Contemporary Speech, *HopKins & Whitaker*
Creative Speaking, *Frank*
Dynamics of Speech, *Myers & Herndon*
Getting Started in Oral Interpretation, *Naegelin & Krikac*
Getting Started in Public Speaking, *Carlin & Payne*
Listening by Doing, *Galvin*
Literature Alive, *Gamble & Gamble*
Person to Person, *Galvin & Book*
Public Speaking Today, *Carlin & Payne*
Speaking by Doing, *Buys, Sill, & Beck*

Theatre
Acting & Directing, *Grandstaff*
The Book of Cuttings for Acting & Directing, *Cassady*
The Book of Monologues for Aspiring Actors, *Cassady*
The Book of Scenes for Acting Practice, *Cassady*
The Book of Scenes for Aspiring Actors, *Cassady*
The Dynamics of Acting, *Snyder & Drumsta*
Getting Started in Theatre, *Pinnell*
An Introduction to Modern One-Act Plays, *Cassady*
An Introduction to Theatre and Drama, *Cassady & Cassady*
Play Production Today, *Beck et al.*
Stagecraft, *Beck*

For a current catalog and information about our complete line of
language arts books, write:
National Textbook Company
a division of NTC Publishing Group
4255 West Touhy Avenue
Lincolnwood (Chicago), Illinois 60646-1975 U.S.A.